D0206136

THE MUSIC OF ARTHUR SULLIVAN

THE MUSIC
OF
ARTHUR SULLIVAN

BY

GERVASE HUGHES
M.A., B.MUS. (OXON.)

GREENWOOD PRESS, PUBLISHERS
WESTPORT, CONNECTICUT

750478

Library of Congress Cataloging in Publication Data

Hughes, Gervase.
The music of Arthur Sullivan.

Reprint of the 1960 ed. published by Macmillan,
London.
1. Sullivan, Sir Arthur Seymour, 1842-1900.
I. Title.
ML410.S95H8 1973   782.8'1'0924   73-9128
ISBN 0-8371-6985-2

Copyright © Gervase Hughes 1959

Originally published in 1960 by Macmillan & Company, Ltd.,
London, St. Martin's Press, New York

Reprinted with the permission of St. Martin's Press

Reprinted in 1973 by Greenwood Press,
a division of Williamhouse-Regency Inc.

Library of Congress Catalogue Card Number 73-9128

ISBN 0-8371-6985-2

Printed in the United States of America

FOREWORD

ANYONE wishing to make a fair assessment of Arthur Sullivan's contribution to music faces some initial obstacles. Although even detractors concede that his orchestration is admirable, comparatively little of his considerable output has been published in full score ; a list would include about half the choral and orchestral works, but only three out of twenty-two completed operas.[1] Most of the music on which his popularity depends is thus not readily available except in piano arrangements, which sometimes give an incomplete or even misleading idea of the composer's intentions. Of the rest much is out of print, and at least half a dozen large-scale works have never been published at all.

My warm thanks are therefore due to Miss Bridget d'Oyly Carte, to Sir Ernest Bullock (Director of the Royal College of Music), to Messrs. Charles Russell & Company (Solicitors) and to Mr. Howard G. Dunkley (a trustee of the late Herbert Sullivan's estate), through whose courtesy I have had the opportunity of consulting orchestral manuscripts not normally accessible. This has enabled me to discuss Sullivan's scoring in greater detail than would otherwise have been possible and to quote from unpublished works which have not been played within living memory and can rarely have been studied, but which nevertheless have their significance in his development.

[1] *Viz. H.M.S. Pinafore* with a German text entitled *Amor an Bord* (Litolff), *The Mikado* (Bosworth) and *Ivanhoe* (Chappell). For many years it was believed that all copies of *Amor an Bord* had been lost or destroyed, but one was recently traced in the United States and is now in the British Museum. Students will find a few discrepancies, for it accords with the original vocal score which was sent to the printers well before the first performance ; later editions incorporate Sullivan's last-minute alterations.

Research that might well have been tedious was expedited by the co-operation of the staff at the d'Oyly Carte office, headed by Mr. Frederic Lloyd and Mr. Stanley H. Parker ; I am grateful to them for their hospitality as well as for much useful information.

An adequate acknowledgment of what I owe to Dr. Eric Blom would have caused him acute embarrassment ; today, unhappily, I write with no fear of offending his modesty. Though the debt cannot be paid I can at least record the obligation. As a firm friend he encouraged with generous enthusiasm my proposal to analyse the qualities of a composer who occupied a small but warm corner in his own affections ; as a fine scholar he drew my attention to features I might otherwise have overlooked. Later, he read the typescript and made a host of pertinent suggestions ; many were argued over in conversation or correspondence, the discussions being enlivened by his learned, witty, outspoken pronouncements on topics that ranged far beyond the matter in hand. Had Eric Blom lived to read the little book he helped on its way, he might from time to time have murmured ' *De gustibus . . .* ', but I think he would have been pleased to light on a phrase here or a comment there which could be promptly traced back to those stimulating exchanges.

GERVASE HUGHES

May 1959

CONTENTS

'Die Natur müsste zerbersten, wollte sie lauter Beethovens gebären.'

ROBERT SCHUMANN, *Die neue Zeitschrift*, Vol. 7

CHAPTER I

INTRODUCTORY

THE shelves of our public libraries are loaded with books about the Gilbert-and-Sullivan operas written by men and women justly proud of their association with the author, the composer, or the D'Oyly Carte Opera Company which has upheld the tradition. Some of them are quite entertaining, and in the store-house of trivial recollection, society gossip and dressing-room tittle-tattle, one occasionally comes across an illuminating anecdote. But sentences like 'Gilbert said he quite agreed with me' and 'Sir Arthur would not have stood it for a moment' make the *primum mobile* all too clear.

Not all the bibliography, of course, falls into this category. For instance, *The Gilbert and Sullivan Operas*, by H. M. Walbrook (1921), is a charmingly written, though rather superficial synopsis. *Gilbert and Sullivan*, by A. H. Godwin (1926), investigates their characteristics more thoroughly, but the enthusiasm sometimes outruns objectivity. Another book with the same title by Hesketh Pearson (1935) is a penetrating study of two conflicting yet complementary personalities. (Pearson's *Gilbert, his life and strife*, published as recently as 1957, is largely a development of the same theme, but it tells us little more about Sullivan, either as man or collaborator.) *The World of Gilbert and Sullivan*, by W. A Darlington (1950), although mainly concerned with Gilbert's technique as a playwright, contains a few shrewd comments on the music, as does *Gilbert and Sullivan Opera* (1953) in which Audrey Williamson analyses the 'tradition'; her considered judgments on past and present standards of performance in both theatre and recording studio are very much to the point.

Any musical criticism there may be in *Sir Arthur Sullivan* by Herbert Sullivan (his nephew) and Newman Flower (1927) is at second hand — extracts from contemporary press reports, etc. This is the 'official' biography; it is useful for checking references and includes an invaluable chronological list of Sullivan's compositions compiled by a librarian of the British Museum. The account it gives of his life and activities, however, is not sufficiently detached to carry conviction; the relevant sections of Leslie Baily's well-documented *Gilbert and Sullivan Book* (1952) give a truer picture of the composer's character. The 'gossipy' and biographical books, taken collectively, have done Sullivan a disservice by their lack of frankness and — in one connection at least — their failure to preserve a sense of proportion. While we learn far more than we need to know about his student flirtations in Leipzig, his early and unfortunate love-affair with Rosamund Barnett and his innocent Indian summer with 'Miss Violet', we find only a few references — mostly very discreet — to his long association with the beautiful Mrs. Ronalds, who played a large part in shaping his career from their first meeting in 1877 until his death in 1900. It was she who encouraged him to devote his talents to operetta rather than oratorio, who helped to smooth over many differences with Gilbert, who accompanied him to rehearsals and auditions (where her presence was often resented by the singers), and who remained at his side during the last pathetic years when health and inspiration alike were failing. As guide, philosopher and something more than friend, her influence was tremendous. Hesketh Pearson and Leslie Baily, to their credit, make no bones about the nature of the relationship, and there should never have been any reason to pretend that it was purely platonic.

Yet Sullivan the man has received fairer treatment than Sullivan the musician. As a matter of course his achievements have been summarised in reference books and their value estimated (differently) in various musical histories and encyclopaedias. From time to time, too, leading professional critics have taken advantage of a revival or an anniversary to discuss a particular work in detail or make a general reassessment. So far, so good; when it comes to full-length studies it is another story. The few publications that date round the turn of the century, mostly written by personal acquaintances, display so little true aesthetic insight and are so stuffed with undiscriminating eulogy that they can be disregarded by a serious researcher. *Sullivan*, by H. Saxe Wyndham (1926), is admittedly a much better balanced appraisement, but has the layman's approach and contains little perceptive criticism. More recently we have had a discerning but all-too-short monograph, *Gilbert and Sullivan*, written by Arthur Jacobs in 1951 for the 'World of Music' series, and practical instruction for aspiring musical directors (*Training the Gilbert and Sullivan Chorus*, by William Cox-Ife, 1955). But only one volume has appeared that is truly worthy of the subject — *Sullivan's Comic Operas*, by Thomas Dunhill, published in 1929. Even this, as its title implies, is limited in scope.

Like so many others before and since, Dunhill was led to music by an early love for Sullivan (as a boy he attended more than one 'first night' at the Savoy), and he never lost his fervour. When he entered the Royal College of Music in 1893 Sullivan's old friend Sir George Grove was still Director, but under his successor Dunhill found the surroundings less congenial. 'It was considered scarcely decent to mention Sullivan's name with approval in the building.' Dunhill stuck to his guns, and when he later returned to the R.C.M. as a member of the teaching staff he continued to fire them in an atmosphere that remained antipathetic. Since those days — thanks in no small degree to his own marksmanship — the climate of musical opinion has warmed considerably towards Sullivan, so that Dunhill's book suffers in retrospect from having been written 'mainly in defence' (to quote his own first chapter-heading).

Defence involved retaliation, and in his counter-attack on Ernest Walker's notorious diatribe in *A History of Music in England* his bullets sometimes flew wide of the target. Here is Walker:

> Not infrequently (especially in the concerted music, such as the madrigal from *The Mikado*) we have something which . . . is the work of a genuine and delicate-handed artist.

Commenting on this passage Dunhill doubts whether the 'well-known Oxford musician . . . speaks from actual knowledge [since he finds nothing] worthy of praise in addition to one little vocal quartet'. Now if words mean anything the madrigal was not cited as an *isolated* instance but as an *example* of the artistic touch which the author found 'not infrequently'. Again, Dunhill took strong exception to the contemptuous expressions applied to *Ivanhoe* and the oratorios, but did he not in his heart endorse them? At any rate he went so far as to write: 'We shall not determine the true importance of Sullivan until we make up our minds to disregard his serious work altogether', when obviously what he meant was that for Sullivan's sake he *preferred* to disregard it. And by taking short extracts out of context he sought to prove Walker guilty of 'what is perhaps the most offensive crime of the critic, to pronounce sentence of death without listening to evidence in favour of the accused'. Surely this was being as unfair to Walker as Walker himself was to Sullivan.

That Walker *was* unfair is now almost universally acknowledged. His faint praise was continually tempered with damning qualifications which let his prejudices out of the bag — 'in its trifling way', 'in its slight way', 'when he is at his best', and so on. It is a pity that Dunhill did not live to read J. A. Westrup's revised version of *A History of Music in England*, for he would have enjoyed the humorous conceit which adapted Walker's own phrases to reach an antithetical conclusion, thus demonstrating the *volte-face* of the academic attitude.

Ernest Walker (1907)	*Ernest Walker, revised* [sic] *by J. A. Westrup* (1952)
The impress he has left on one department of English music is undoubtedly very deep, though it may not prove lasting. The comic operas written to the libretti of W. S. Gilbert made his reputation and indeed form his chief title to fame ; though we cannot forget how enormous a share of the success they enjoyed was due to the brilliant sparkling wit of his collaborator.	The impress that he left on one department of English music was undoubtedly very deep. The comic operas written to the libretti of W. S. Gilbert made his reputation and indeed form his chief title to fame. Though we cannot forget that a considerable share of the success they achieved was due to the brilliant sparkling wit of his collaborator, it has become increasingly evident that they survive by virtue of the music.

(One regrets that Professor Westrup saw fit to retain Walker's cruel final paragraph, in which Sullivan is summarily dismissed as 'a popularity-hunting trifler'.)

But to return to Dunhill. If one can overlook the smarting sense of vicarious injustice under which he laboured (and to which from today's standpoint he would seem to have been unnecessarily sensitive), one finds his self-styled 'critical appreciation' enthusiastic but unbiased, concise but not unduly compressed, and scholarly without being touched by intellectual snobbery. Unfortunately it is out of print, but it remains — with the possible exceptions of Jacobs' tiny treatise and Cox-Ife's text-book — the only work entirely devoted to Sullivan written by a trained musician equipped with sincerity and discrimination. He succeeded admirably in presenting Sullivan to the public as something more than a purveyor of pretty tunes, and served his own profession well by proving that a composer of light music was not necessarily unworthy of being taken seriously.

Dunhill's achievement was that of a pioneer, a preliminary skirmish in a campaign whose advance has yet to be implemented. Today there may be few musicians for whom — as for Ernest Walker — Sullivan is merely 'the idle singer of an empty evening'; there are many who, while acknowledging his great gifts, tend to take them for granted. One recalls Schumann's curiously aloof attitude to Haydn : 'he is like a familiar friend of the house whom all greet with pleasure and with esteem, but who has ceased to arouse any particular interest'. But the new generation, though it may sometimes look back in anger, prefers to look forward in hope; Sullivan has started countless young people along the enchanted road that leads to the Elysian Fields, and they need not only encouragement but help. The time is surely ripe for a comprehensive study of his music as a whole which, while recognising that the operettas 'form his chief title to fame' will not leave the rest out of account, and while taking note of his weaknesses (which are many) and not hesitating to castigate his lapses from good taste (which were comparatively rare) will attempt to view them in perspective against the wider background of his sound musicianship.

Those who find it difficult to thread their way through technical labyrinths will take short cuts, which need not preclude the discovery that enjoyment of a Sullivan operetta, as of a Beethoven symphony, can be heightened by knowing the 'how' and the 'why', for Sullivan's adroit approach is well worth attention, and in one or two respects his methods differ from those of any other composer; therein, partly, lies his genius. To relate his achievements to those of Mozart would be ridiculous, and comparison with the later Verdi would not redound to his advantage, yet thanks to his resource in such matters *Iolanthe* and *The Gondoliers* do *belong to the world* of *Così fan tutte* and *Falstaff* — not to that of *Orphée aux enfers* and *The Merry Widow*.

This is a book about Sullivan's *music*; all else is incidental. To set the scene, however, Chapters II and III incorporate a short biographical survey which will provide a chronological basis for what follows. Readers who have vocal scores may like to keep them handy for reference, for the operas will not be separately summarised although each will be documented in the index.

And now a word on the subject of generic nomenclature. The collaborators themselves dubbed their offerings with a fine disregard for consistency.[1] It would be better to agree once and for all that they are in fact 'operettas', and in this commentary operettas they shall be, rather than 'comic operas', whenever it is necessary to differentiate the genre. But in nine cases out of ten no such nice distinction is involved, and to call them anything but 'operas' would then be as pedantic as to insist that *Seraglio* should always be a ' *Singspiel*' and *Parsifal* always a 'music-drama'. In any case it is as 'operas' that *H.M.S. Pinafore* and *The Yeomen of the Guard* are part of our national heritage; long may they remain so.

[1] *Trial by Jury*, for instance, was a 'Dramatic Cantata' and *Ruddigore* an 'Entirely Original Supernatural Opera'. Abroad, misunderstandings arose; the French musicologist Arthur Pougin, in the standard *Biographie universelle des musiciens* (1880), wrote: 'Entre autres ouvrages, on lui doit encore deux cantates : le Jugement du jury, et Sur terre et nor'. (For the latter, see page 16.)

CHAPTER II

THE FIRST PERIOD

ARTHUR SEYMOUR SULLIVAN was born at Lambeth, London, on 13th May 1842. His parents were both of Irish descent although not actually born in Ireland. His mother had Italian blood in her veins, and it was from her that young Arthur inherited his black hair, dark eyes and olive-tinted complexion. His father, a clarinet-player and later a military bandmaster, fostered his natural aptitude for music, taught him much about orchestral instruments and arranged for his voice to be trained at the Chapel Royal, where he was soon encouraged to try his hand at composition. In 1856 he became the first holder of the Mendelssohn Scholarship at the Royal Academy of Music. His progress was so satisfactory that the committee also paid his fees for two years at the Leipzig Conservatorium. In the event he stayed in Germany a further six months at his father's expense.

The only work of any consequence written during his student days was the music for Shakespeare's *Tempest*, which had its first performance at Leipzig in April 1861. As might be expected, immaturity showed itself in a mixture of styles. The introduction here and there suggests Beethoven.

The third-act prelude and the Banquet Dance, though well

constructed, might have been written by any one of half a dozen contemporary German composers, Jensen for instance. The fourth-act prelude is a light-hearted compound of the last movement of Schumann's first symphony and the first movement of his last, with a sprightly second subject — more Italian than German in character — thrown in for good measure (see Ex. 111, page 107). Finally, the Nymphs' and Reapers' Dance (see Ex. 136, page 118) is a sparkling scherzo in the best Mendelssohn tradition. Curiously there are few traces of Schubert's influence in *The Tempest*. Sullivan's mentors at Leipzig were not very broad-minded; although they worshipped Mendelssohn and admired Schumann, they despised French music as effeminate and may have mistaken the frank *bonhomie* of the Austrian 'upstart' for triviality. Sullivan outdid them in his enthusiasm for Schumann, and after his return to London was an ardent champion of that composer (whose music had as yet made no impact in this country); if he ever shared their views on Paris and Vienna he soon made amends.

For the next six years he settled down to earn a living by teaching and organ-playing. He had an attractive personality and quickly established some useful contacts in the musical and literary world, notably with George Grove (then secretary of the Crystal Palace Concerts Society), H. F. Chorley (the leading music critic of the day), Michael Costa (director of the Royal Italian Opera, Covent Garden) and F. C. Burnand (editor of *Punch*).

With Chorley he started work on an opera, *The Sapphire Necklace*, which was never completed (but see Ex. 70 on page 76 for a quotation). For Costa he wrote a ballet, *L'Ile enchantée*. Of two numbers only is there a (copied) manuscript score in existence, but all the string parts still survive, and, furthermore, some of the music was used over again in later works, so that it has been possible to form an opinion on its quality as a whole. It is less pretentious and more homogeneous than *The Tempest*, but technically shows no advance.

Presently Sullivan succumbed to the spell of Schubert's genius and Gounod's sensual charm. Both these influences can be traced in the masque *Kenilworth* (words again by Chorley but incorporating a good deal of Shakespeare), which was produced at the Birmingham Festival of 1864. The most ambitious item was a romantic duet 'How sweet the moonlight sleeps upon this bank'. One stanza, beginning with the words 'Look, how the floor of heaven', is remarkable in that it consists of four five-bar phrases, and the final section ('In such a night as this') is freely rhapsodical. This was an exceptional effort, for in his early days the verses that Sullivan chose to set to music generally stifled rather than stimulated his flow of melody and aptitude for rhythmic originality. He was imprisoned in a square cage of strophic restrictions from which he rarely broke free, and Orpheus' Lute was never used to better purpose than when it secured him a day's liberty.

Reverting to *Kenilworth*, mention must be made of the Slow Dance, an early-eighteenth-century pastiche where Sullivan for the first time captured a truly English atmosphere. Here is its ending — note how the phrases fall into irregular bar-lengths and resolve naturally in the characteristic overlapping 2/4 of the cadence.

In the introduction to his *Symphony in E* (1866) the same cross-rhythm appears in very different guise; this time one thinks of Schumann again, perhaps even of Brahms, whose early compositions (including the D minor piano concerto) Sullivan had doubtless heard in Germany.

Unfortunately the first subject proper, a violin *cantabile* of soaring promise, falls to pieces at the seventh bar. (It shows its paces satisfactorily in the development section, however.)

Although the second subject is a mere fragment, sonata form is competently handled, and the whole movement, if rising to no great heights, comes up to one's expectations. The lyrical second movement, where an expressive theme is inadequately supported by a rather jejune accompaniment, is in B major; a long oboe solo (see Ex. 103, page 103) links it with the third, which eventually gets off the mark in the unrelated key of C major. This has the unconventional formal pattern ABCA — cf. the scherzo from Tchaikovsky's no. 4 — with a tiny coda based on B to round things off. (A and B are in 2/4 time, C in 3/4.) The naïve melodies are rigidly four-square, and in one of them the echo of Schubert is almost comical (Ex. 5).

The lively tripping measures of the finale tend to outstay their welcome, perhaps because the orchestration is less skilful than usual, with the melodic interest largely confined to the first violins. In spite of the promising first movement and a modicum of competent thematic development, the symphony cannot be counted as a satisfactory achievement. Too much of the material is machine-made — as yet we find few signs of true spontaneity.

Perhaps only once during Sullivan's youth did music really come from the heart — when a few months after the symphony the sudden death of his father impelled him to pour forth his feelings in the *In Memoriam* overture. The superscription is misleading, for at the head of a published work it implies commemoration of an event more widely significant than a family bereavement, however distressing. The music is indeed purely subjective; Sullivan might be able to convey his mental reaction in terms of crotchets and quavers but it was beyond his powers to project an emotional experience into the consciousness of a detached audience. After all, he was only twenty-four, and if the opening melody strikes a sophisticated ear as being inadequately expressive of even personal grief, there is no need to laugh at those who find its obvious sincerity rather touching. Taken as a whole, *In Memoriam* has a solid dignity that is quite impressive; it deserves to be played now and again, but emphatically not — *pace* Sir Henry Wood —

to mark Remembrance Day or on solemn occasions of national mourning.

To this period, too, belong the *Cello Concerto* (a manuscript I have been unable to locate) and the *Marmion* overture, which is as substantial as *In Memoriam* and rather reminiscent of Mendelssohn's *Ruy Blas*, though less obviously ingratiating; it might well bear revival, for the orchestration is exceptionally fine — see Ex. 93 on page 99.

In 1867 Sullivan wrote two miniature operas with Burnand as librettist. The best numbers from *Cox and Box* and *The Contrabandista* have an engaging simplicity that suggests Offenbach, but neither would be remembered had he not later enjoyed such triumphs in the same genre. At the time he took far more seriously his visit to Vienna with George Grove. At the back of a dusty cupboard in the house of a certain Dr. Schneider they found the manuscript parts of the *Rosamunde* music, much of it given up for lost, which had lain there undisturbed since its production forty-four years earlier. Sullivan's share in this discovery gave him lasting pleasure.

Soon he gave up his organist's post, for by this time he had lighted on a more lucrative occupation — the turning out of anthems, hymn-tunes, part-songs and above all drawing-room ballads, for which there was evidently an insatiable demand. The space taken up by such trifles in a list of his compositions for the years 1867 to 1874 inclusive is out of all proportion to their worth. There is a nostalgic charm about *Oh hush thee, my baby* and *The long day closes*, which are still popular with small choral societies, but it is to be hoped that Adelaide Procter's elusive Chord has now been Lost for ever. As for such deplorable effusions as *Sad Memories, Looking back* and *Once Again*, the very titles save us from the necessity for comment, since they are only too indicative of the depths to which Sullivan could fall when he wanted to keep his pot on the boil.

He pulled himself together for *The Window* (1871), a song-cycle with words by Tennyson, in which he once more acknow-ledged his debt to Schubert with the simple but entirely satisfying arpeggio accompaniment of 'Gone', and an occasional characteristic modulation. Here are a few bars from 'On the hill'.

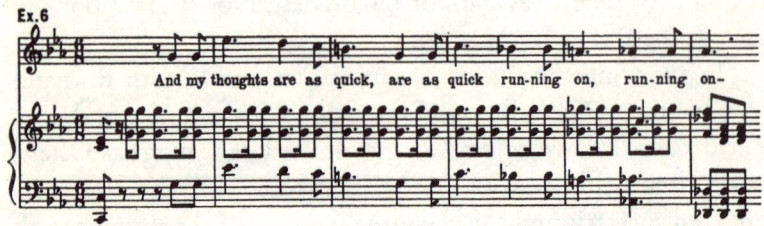

And my thoughts are as quick, are as quick run-ning on, run-ning on-

His finest work of these years, and indeed one of the best pieces of light music ever written for orchestra alone, is the captivating *Di Ballo* overture (1870). Nothing quite like it has ever happened before or since ; it is as clear-cut as the over-ture to *La gazza ladra*, as tuneful as the overture to *The Merry Wives of Windsor*, as varied as the overture to *Die Fledermaus*, as exuberant as *España*, as refined as *Masques et bergamasques*, as vital as *Cockaigne*. If Sullivan did not achieve Rossini's classical touch, Nicolai's *savoir-faire*, Johann Strauss' rhythmic verve, Chabrier's orchestral brilliance, Fauré's subtlety or Elgar's technical mastery, he nevertheless here first carved his name on the pedestal of fame. For all the overture's familiarity one point sometimes escapes notice — that the scintillating *galop* is a syncopated metamorphosis of the graceful waltz that has done such excellent duty as second subject in the preceding sonata-form section. The first subject from the symphony (Ex. 4, page 11) should be compared with this theme from *Di Ballo*, which starts very similarly and is also a twelve-bar phrase, but which maintains interest instead of allowing it to lapse — note especially the effective *sforzando* on an unaccented bar.

Few of the other early orchestral works require comment. The incidental music to *The Merchant of Venice* (1871) includes a bourrée which is another pastiche, longer, more elaborate and better known than the Slow Dance from *Kenilworth*, and a waltz which successfully recaptures for a few moments the mood of *Di Ballo*. (There is a short quotation from the bourrée in Ex. 68 on page 75 and from the waltz in Ex. 118 on page 109.) Presently Sullivan's commitments began to pile up, and and it was with reluctance that in 1874 he consented to provide music for another Shakespearean production, *The Merry Wives of Windsor*. Eventually this was limited to the scene in Windsor Forest which other composers, before and since, have found a fruitful source of inspiration. Sullivan, pressed for time, lifted great chunks from *L'Ile enchantée* for the purpose, but in one of the few new numbers (Ex. 8a) he caught the magic of the atmosphere and actually foreshadowed Verdi's treatment (Ex. 8b).

Ex.8b (Falstaff, Act III)

Chorus Piz-zi-ca, piz-zi-ca, l'unghia vin-tuz-zo-la! piz-zi-ca, piz-zi-ca, l'unghia vin-tuz-zo-la!

In serious concerted music he had yet to find his feet. It is in vain that we search the pages of *The Prodigal Son* (1869) for any sign of initiative; one of the first choruses is a setting of the words 'Let us eat and drink, for tomorrow we die', and as we wade through the rest of the work, half-submerged in a bog of conventional clichés, this strikes us as having been sound advice. *The Light of the World* (1873) is not much better, but the orchestral interlude entitled 'Pastoral Symphony' possibly deserves to be rescued from its surroundings. Whatever to-day's judgment may be, however, these oratorios—and the mildly picturesque cantata *On Shore and Sea* (1871)—were suited to the fashion of their time, and Sullivan soon became a popular figure in high society, hob-nobbing on terms of equality with the Prince of Wales, the Duke of Edinburgh, the ex-Empress Eugénie, *et hoc genus omne*.

But the most important event of this period was his meeting with W. S. Gilbert, six years his senior and already well known as the author of *Bab Ballads* and several plays. Their first joint-offspring, *Thespis* (1871), survived for only a month or two; nearly all the music has been lost. In 1875, however, a very shrewd impressario — Richard d'Oyly Carte by name — persuaded the two men to collaborate again in a one-act piece to share the bill with Offenbach's *La Périchole*. *Trial by Jury* was a tremendous success, and Sullivan was so bitten by the stage bug that at the request of another manager he dashed off *The Zoo*, with a librettist whose identity it would be kinder not to reveal since he afterwards did good work under a *nom-de-plume*. *The Zoo* achieved a few performances but was never published.

One significant feature will be referred to in Chapter VIII; meanwhile a brief quotation will indicate the quality of words and music.

Ex.9

I loved her fond - ly, and Her fath-er had been＿ a gro-cer,
But when I sought her hand He has-ti-ly ans - wered "No sir."

Not even the wand'ring minstrel could match such flights of poesy, and Sullivan quickly decided to throw in his lot definitely with Carte and Gilbert. It was the turning-point of his career.

COMPARATIVE CHRONOLOGICAL TABLE
OF FIRST PERFORMANCES

Operas and Operettas by Sullivan (complete list)	Contemporary Operas and Operettas by other Composers
	1866 The Bartered Bride
	La Vie parisienne
	Mignon
1867 Cox and Box	1867 Don Carlos
The Contrabandista	The Grand Duchess of Gerolstein
	Romeo and Juliet
	1868 Die Meistersinger
	La Périchole
	1869 Das Rheingold
1871 Thespis	1870 Die Walküre
	1872 Aida
	La Fille de Madame Angot
1875 Trial by Jury	1874 Die Fledermaus
The Zoo	1875 Carmen
	1876 Siegfried
	Götterdämmerung
1877 The Sorcerer	1877 Les Cloches de Corneville
	Samson and Delilah
1878 H.M.S. Pinafore	1878 The Peasant a Rogue
1879 The Pirates of Penzance	1879 Eugen Onegin
1881 Patience	1881 The Tales of Hoffmann
1882 Iolanthe	1882 The Snow Maiden
	Parsifal
1884 Princess Ida	1883 Lakmé
The Sorcerer (revised version)	1884 Manon
1885 The Mikado	1885 The Gipsy Baron
	1886 Dorothy
1887 Ruddigore	1887 Otello
1888 The Yeomen of the Guard	1890 Cavalleria rusticana
1889 The Gondoliers	La Basoche
	Prince Igor
1891 Ivanhoe	The Queen of Spades
1892 Haddon Hall	1892 Pagliacci
	The Mountebanks
1893 Utopia Limited	1893 Falstaff
	Manon Lescaut
	Hänsel und Gretel
1895 The Chieftain	1894 Thaïs
1896 The Grand Duke	1896 Shamus O'Brien
	The Geisha
1898 The Beauty Stone	La Bohème
1899 The Rose of Persia	1898 Véronique

CHAPTER III

SULLIVAN AND GILBERT

THE partnership flourished from 1877 until 1890. Almost annually London was treated to another 'Gilbert-and-Sullivan' under Carte's management — *The Sorcerer, H.M.S. Pinafore, The Pirates of Penzance* and *Patience* at the old Opera Comique; then *Iolanthe, Princess Ida, The Mikado, Ruddigore, The Yeomen of the Guard* and *The Gondoliers* at the Savoy. The *least* successful ran for 247 performances[1] and two knocked on 700, a very rare achievement in the eighteen-eighties. Many of Sullivan's serious-minded contemporaries looked askance at such meretricious triumphs; they reserved their applause for two cantatas written at the request of the Leeds Festival Committee — *The Martyr of Antioch* (1880) and *The Golden Legend* (1886) — which, apart from the *Macbeth* music (1888), were virtually his only other compositions during these thirteen years.[2]

It was a busy time for Sullivan. He had to fulfil conducting engagements all over Great Britain, and paid two extended visits to the United States. For several years, too, he was Director of the newly founded National Training School for Music in South Kensington (later the Royal College of Music) and President of the Birmingham and Midland Institute; the duties may not have been onerous, but he seems to have carried

---

[1] *The Sorcerer* was played only 175 times at the Opera Comique, but it was given again at the Savoy 'with alterations and additions' to fill the gap between *Princess Ida* and *The Mikado* and thereby reached the 300 mark.

[2] Sullivan described *The Martyr of Antioch* as a 'Sacred Music Drama' and later adapted it for a stage production by the Carl Rosa Opera Company, but it cannot properly be regarded as belonging to any but the 'cantata' category.

them out conscientiously. Between-whiles he indulged his favourite hobbies — horse-racing, roulette and the cultivation of royalty (he was knighted in 1883). It is astonishing that his constitution stood the strain. Never strong physically, from about 1873 onwards he had been increasingly troubled with stone in the kidney; twice at least he nearly died of this painful disease.

The music of Sullivan's maturity will be fully discussed in later chapters, but one point of over-riding significance must be stressed here and now. The best of his early works had owed their good qualities to his familiarity with the eighteenth-century classics and his sincere admiration for Schubert, Mendelssohn and other illustrious composers of the early nineteenth, yet his subsequent development was even more profoundly influenced by a man whose only claim to be a musician was that he recognised *God Save the Queen* when he heard it. Hitherto much of Sullivan's output — especially the vocal and concerted pieces — had been marred by too easy an acceptance of current convention, and it was the originality, wit and, above all, metrical ingenuity of Gilbert's verses that gave him the driving-power that he so badly needed. *Cox and Box* had been an innocent mid-Victorian frolic to which he had contributed his modest share of homely fun; the brilliant libretto of *Trial by Jury* inspired him to play his full part in the creation of a comic masterpiece which, for all its imperfections, remains unsurpassed as a curtain-raiser to this day. Here author and composer played generously into each other's hands and between them they won nearly all the tricks.

It was indeed a fertile *liaison*, for if Gilbert planted the seed from which many of the best melodies sprang, Sullivan breathed life into doggerel rhymes that would have stood no chance of independent survival. And how often they hit on the unforgettable phrase in which words and music are for ever inseparable ! Though both were addicted to sentimentality, in their combined work the lapses were comparatively few and did not always coincide. Sullivan let Gilbert down rather badly in one or two of the tenor songs, but elsewhere he more than restored the balance by fitting exquisite music to some very second-rate lyrics.

More often than not, however, their humour and sentiment marched together, and they were absolutely at one in their sympathetic portrayal of that innocent gaiety which we are asked to believe was such a pleasing characteristic of Victorian maidens. Hence the consistently high standard of words and music in the ensembles where pretty girls play a leading part; none are mawkish, nearly all are charming, and a few deserve even higher commendation. In 'Comes a train of little ladies' (*The Mikado*) both men excelled themselves. It is a supreme example of their happy collaboration in capturing an atmosphere of youthful femininity trembling deliciously on the threshold of womanhood. The full beauty of this lovely chorus can only be appreciated in an actual performance, but I cannot forbear to quote the last few bars.

Perfection was not attained without much heart-searching. Sullivan, for instance, by no means shared Gilbert's fondness for poking fun at the fading charms of middle-aged spinsters, and sometimes turned the tables neatly by setting satirical words with apparent sincerity — as in Lady Jane's song from *Patience*. Although some critics, notably Sir Arthur Quiller-Couch, have lost their sense of proportion in condemning such characterisations as 'sadistic', this sort of thing weighed heavily on Sullivan, which was one reason (there were others) why in 1884 he rejected the draft libretto of *The Mountebanks* (later most admirably put to music by Alfred Cellier) where certainly Gilbert more than once overstepped the bounds of good taste.

This decision irritated Gilbert and worried Carte, for it was symptomatic of Sullivan's growing discontent. He was tired of setting jingles and hankered to re-establish himself as a serious composer by writing a grand opera; this time it was Gilbert who refused to take part — it would only emphasise his subordinate position as a mere hack which, as an established playwright, he was already finding intolerable. He himself thought a lot of his own plays and resented it when others did not share that opinion; in truth they were mostly fustian, being often written in the blankest of blank verse, and it was only after joining forces with Sullivan that he brought to the stage his talent for clever rhyming, pointed wit and — occasionally — tender charm. Thus neither Gilbert nor Sullivan escaped the pangs of jealousy, for the subconscious realisation of their interdependence caused each to grudge the other his share in their joint success. There were continual arguments — not all good-tempered — but for many years Carte managed to keep his restless team in harness. When each opera in turn proved itself a money-spinner they were certainly fulsome in their mutual congratulations; hard words were forgiven and differences forgotten — until the next production was due.

Partly it was a clash of personalities. Gilbert's caustic jibes and studied rudeness were a façade; in spite of a predilection for Rabelaisian humour in the smoking-room and innocent flirtation in the salon, he adhered to a rigid, almost puritanical pattern of life and devoted himself to his work with a steadiness of artistic purpose which was never one of Sullivan's attributes. He respected and indeed admired his colleague for his achievements in the world of music, but he had little sympathy with the bohemian *bon viveur* who composed his operas in feverish spasms, sometimes finishing them on the morning of the first performance. As time went on the edifice Carte had so painstakingly built up showed further signs of strain; disagreements became more frequent and recriminations more violent — a break sooner or later seemed inevitable. When it came, however, it was a matter of business, not incompatibility, that was the immediate cause. Returning from a holiday abroad early in 1890, Gilbert found that in the expense account for *The Gondoliers* Carte had debited Sullivan and himself with the cost (£500) of new carpets for the foyer of the Savoy Theatre. This spark set his fiery temper ablaze; although the heat was turned primarily on Carte, Sullivan's attempts at mediation merely served to fan a flame that soon scorched them both.

We are concerned here not with the rights and wrongs of this famous quarrel (eventually fought out in the law courts) but with its effect on the relationship of the three participants. The first casualties were Gilbert's manners, Sullivan's health, and Carte's judgment. 'I'll beat you both yet, you scoundrels!' roared the blustering author; 'I am mentally and physically ill over this wretched business,' complained the sensitive composer; estranged from Gilbert, the sanguine impresario placed too much reliance on Sullivan's initiative. Carte's logic was sound as far as it went: in spite of the rising tension Sullivan had not only retained his flair for setting light verses but had gradually brought to this type of work a widened outlook and improved technique so that almost every opera from *Pinafore* onwards had been musically superior to its predecessor; even if new librettists had to be found they could hardly fail to be more congenial than Gilbert; why should not the glass continue to rise? But alas, Gilbert's understudies proved broken reeds, and the steady mercurial ascent to the pinnacle of *The Gondoliers* was followed by a sudden deep depression; the stimulus Sullivan needed had been withdrawn.

His long-awaited grand opera aroused great hopes. In the event it had been written by Julian Sturgis and composed during the height of the carpet controversy; Her Majesty the Queen had been graciously pleased to accept the dedication. But *Ivanhoe* (1891) came up to nobody's expectations; Sullivan himself was disillusioned — 'grand opera is the greatest gamble in the world, and a cobbler should stick to his last' he confided to Reginald de Koven, who accompanied him to one of the performances. He struggled hard with some music for *The Foresters*, but Tennyson's uncompromising attitude irked him. So, not surprisingly, did the literary style.

> There is no land like England
> Where'er the light of day be;
> There are no wives like English wives,
> So fair and chaste as they be.

How did the author of *The Idylls of the King* come to put his name to such puerile rubbish? This regrettable affair aroused small enthusiasm in New York and it was never played in London at all. Sullivan had had a lesson and he insisted that his next librettist (Sydney Grundy) should proffer two alternative lyrics for every song in *Haddon Hall* (Gilbert had always been ready to do so on request). Even so the music came slowly during a period of great suffering when, for the third time, he nearly succumbed to his old complaint. Billed as an 'English Light Opera' *Haddon Hall* enjoyed a mild *succès d'estime*, but when the public stayed away Carte saw the red light. He held out a tentative olive-branch to Gilbert, who consented to bury the hatchet on certain conditions; with Sullivan now only too ready to agree, a rather grudging reconciliation was effected and after an interval of four years the curtain went up on a new 'Gilbert-and-Sullivan'.

No expense had been spared to make *Utopia Limited* (1893) a success, and at first it was well received. But the old magic was gone, the nightly takings soon dropped, and by Savoy standards it could only be accounted a failure. Both author and composer accepted the fact, and they turned aside again — Gilbert to an independent theatrical venture and Sullivan to a whirl of social activity. During the next two years music was neglected; for the time being his horses Cranmer and Blue Mark held first place in his affections, though they rarely did so in the races for which they were entered. Only on a long visit to Monte Carlo did he start intermittent work; there he occasionally tore himself away from the casino and bit by bit completed a revised version of his youthful *jeu d'esprit*, *The Contrabandista*. Re-christened *The Chieftain* it achieved a Savoy production, but (like Cranmer and Blue Mark) it had no staying power.

In 1896 Carte brought Gilbert and Sullivan together once again, but *The Grand Duke* was an almighty flop; each blamed the other and the rift between them was now complete. Gilbert retired to his country house at Harrow Weald to nurse his resentment and his gout; Sullivan went for a long holiday to St. Moritz where he enjoyed the company of the Duke and Duchess of Teck, one of whose daughters — later to be Queen of England — gave him 'a beautiful photograph of herself'. His health was now seriously deteriorating, but in return for royal favours he provided some ballet-music for Queen Victoria's Diamond Jubilee (see pages 74, 83) and in 1898 devoted a lot of time to *The Beauty Stone*. Although some of the lyrics had a poetic quality that appealed to him and were certainly better than those of *The Foresters*, Sullivan found the joint authors, Comyns Carr and Arthur Pinero, as unco-operative as Tennyson had been. (A few years previously he had written some very dull music for Comyns Carr's play *King Arthur*.) *The Beauty Stone* was an ineffective piece which survived less than two months and left Sullivan utterly dispirited. During eight years he had tried six new librettists without finding inspiration; 'there is no Sullivan without a Gilbert' was his own comment.

However, his next collaborator, Basil Hood, strove hard to fill the vacancy by cleverly imitative methods, and in *The Rose of Persia* managed to conjure a few sparks of vitality from the flagging composer. This was Carte's most successful new enterprise (financially at any rate) since *The Gondoliers*, and Hood promptly produced another libretto (*The Emerald Isle*) on which Sullivan worked spasmodically (the music was later completed by Edward German). But his physical condition grew gradually worse; another attack of his chronic kidney trouble coincided with a severe throat infection and at times he was in almost unbearable pain. He died on 22nd November 1900.

The news was kept from Carte, who was himself danger-ously ill, but a sixth sense must have told him what had happened. A few days after Sullivan's death he was found lying exhausted on the floor of his Savoy Hotel bedroom, having apparently dragged himself to the window. 'I have seen the last of my old friend Sullivan', he whispered; the funeral procession had indeed just passed along the Embankment on its way to St. Paul's Cathedral.

Although Gilbert never spoke to Sullivan after the fiasco of *The Grand Duke*, he wrote a very cordial letter during the composer's last illness, and had he not been in Egypt recuperating from rheumatic fever there would almost certainly have been a deathbed reunion which — in the popular imagination at least — would have set an appropriate seal on their long, prolific and sometimes turbulent association. Sullivan died too soon to realise that his melodies had conferred immortality on his partner's verses, but as time rolled on and the plays by which he set such store lay neglected and forgotten while the operas continued to flourish, Gilbert began to have an inkling of the truth. In 1903 he wrote to a friend: 'a Gilbert is no use without a Sullivan, and I can't find one' — a pathetic echo of Sullivan's cry five years earlier — and towards the end of his life (he died in 1911) the dictatorial, quick-tempered, warm-hearted old man paid a generous public tribute to his former colleague. 'I am not at my merriest when I remember all that he has done for me in allowing his genius to shed some of its lustre on my humble name.' In return he should be given credit for having rescued Sullivan from a limbo of mediocrity and for stimulating him to put forth music that has brought happiness to countless thousands.

CHAPTER IV

RHYTHM AND WORD-SETTING

WHEN fitting music to words Sullivan usually looked first for any features of rhythmic interest that might be lurking behind the metrical façade, and Gilbert's verses, which often combined a formal balance with strophic irregularity, were a challenge to his ingenuity.

Let us examine his approach to a typical case — Captain Corcoran's song from Act II of *H.M.S. Pinafore*. (One notices at once that the lines have iambic accents 3–3–3–4 in the first two stanzas, 4–4–4–3 in the third, and 3–3–3–4 in the fourth — which is a verbal repetition of the first.)

> Fair moón, to theé I síng!
> Bright régent óf the heávens,
> Say, why' is év'rythíng
> Eithér at síxes ór at sévens?
>
> I háve lived híthertó
> Free fróm the breáth of slánder,
> Belóv'd by áll my créw,
> A reálly pópulár commánder.
>
> But nów my kíndly créw rebél,
> My daúghter tó a tár is pártial,
> Sir Jóseph stórms, and, sád to téll,
> He threátens á court-mártial.
>
> Fair moón, to theé I síng, etc.

When reading this through, Sullivan would disregard the metre and follow the natural syllabic accentuation (*e.g.* 'Eíther at síxes or at sévens '). Then he would jot down half a dozen or so alternative rhythmic outlines, using perhaps three different time-signatures, eventually select one as being the most suitable, and allow it to settle in his subconscious mind while he went off to a race-meeting or a poker-party. Next day, or perhaps a week later, the *melodic* outline would take shape in his *conscious* mind. (As he sometimes had inspirations at socially inconvenient moments, he always carried a small pad of music paper in his pocket, and was even known to interrupt a *tête-à-tête* in order to jot down an idea that had suddenly come to him.) When he next settled to work, he would give the tune a final polish and make a preliminary sketch of the harmony and the instrumental figuration.

This method of composition might not suit everyone but it worked splendidly with Sullivan; to appreciate this, one need only read the lyric once more — as objectively as possible — and compare it line by line with the finished article.

Ex.11

(This extract is necessarily compressed for reasons of space, and the chords are merely intended to indicate the harmonic scheme; the orchestral accompaniment is, of course, more elaborate. That the song ends with a conventional *melisma* superimposed on a hackneyed harmonic progression is here beside the point.)

Phoebe's song 'Were I thy bride' from *The Yeomen of the Guard* is sometimes cited as being a smooth metrical metamorphosis, but in fact it is not really a happy instance. Although the ten-bar setting of the opening is certainly appropriate, the melody charming, the harmonisation fluent, and the orchestral treatment suitably delicate throughout, the retention of an identical time-pattern for each successive stanza (there are eight of them all told) becomes slightly monotonous. Sullivan applied his regular procedure — most successfully — to the first stanza, but thereafter he followed (rhythmically) the line of least resistance.

Other considerations justified a deviation from routine in 'Oh, goddess wise' (*Princess Ida*). Here Sullivan had for once to concentrate on a lyric of true poetic quality, and no other composer would have thought of maintaining a balance by using the same melodic phrase for the final heroic couplet as for the irregular first stanza.

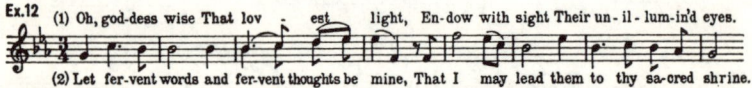

Ex.12 (1) Oh, god-dess wise That lov - est light, En-dow with sight Their un-il-lum-in'd eyes.
(2) Let fer-vent words and fer-vent thoughts be mine, That I may lead them to thy sa-cred shrine.

One only regrets that this led him to a false accent on the word 'to'; apart from a conventional harmonic cliché used in the cadence it is the only blemish (a very minor one) on a beautiful song which does great credit to both author and composer.

Short lines such as occur in these two lyrics are very characteristic of Gilbert's style, and Sullivan enthusiastically explored their potentialities for rhythmic variety. If in due course he lighted on a melody of distinction that fitted the framework he had so carefully chosen, then his music touched the heights. That impeccable song 'The Sun whose rays' (*The Mikado*) comes into this category. Here is the refrain, which incorporates two totally different settings of a single four-line stanza.

A passage from Act I of *The Gondoliers* is also worth quoting, if only as an instance of how Sullivan occasionally allowed his logical approach to carry him near a dangerous extreme. The duet 'We're called *gondolieri*' is followed by two stanzas of five short lines each in which Marco and Giuseppe get down to business. Marco sings the first line 'And now to choose our brides !' in recitative, and then we have this metrical transformation, which is ingenious but hardly gives the rhymes and metre a fair chance.

Such problems are handled even more skilfully (and less drastically) in a self-contained section from the finale of the same act. Gilbert never wrote prettier verses — the first is for the soprano, the second for the soubrette.

1

Now, Marco dear,
My wishes hear:
   While you're away,
It's understood
You will be good
   And not too gay.
To ev'ry trace
Of maiden grace
   You will be blind,
And will not glance
By any chance
   On womankind !
If you are wise
You'll shut your eyes
   Till we arrive,
And not address
A lady less
   Than forty-five.
You'll please to frown
On ev'ry gown
   That you may see;
And, O my pet,
You won't forget
   You've married me !

2

You'll lay your head
Upon your bed
   At set of sun.
You will not sing
Of anything
   To anyone.
You'll sit and mope
All day, I hope,
   And shed a tear
Upon the life
Your little wife
   Is passing here.
And if so be
You think of me,
   Please tell the moon:
I'll read it all
In rays that fall
   On the lagoon:
You'll be so kind
As tell the wind
   How you may be,
And send me words
By little birds
   To comfort me !

And, O my darling, O my pet,
Whatever else you may forget
In yonder isle beyond the sea,
Do not forget you've married me !

Here is the first bar of the music, scored for flutes, clarinet and *pizzicato* violas and basses, with the soprano singing 'Now, Marco dear', etc. on the top line.

Ex.15 Andante con moto

Except for a tiny variation at the words 'And, O my pet', the same rhythm persists until the refrain, which introduces a contrasted *legato* phrase.

In the second verse, by a masterstroke, the accent at the opening is moved by two syllables (*i.e. half* a beat) —

— and presently we have this fascinating evolution.

By the time she reaches 'send me words By little birds' the soubrette is a *whole* beat ahead of the soprano (at the corresponding point of the first verse), and she starts her refrain not only a fourth lower (*i.e.* in the dominant) but *two* beats ahead. A passage remarkable for harmonic subtlety leads back to the tonic, where the voices of tenor and baritone blend with the others in a final repetition of 'O my darling, O my pet', etc. This captivating piece shows Sullivan at his very best (Gilbert, too).

Shifting accents also play their part in another ensemble, more sprightly and equally charming, this time from *The Mikado*; it contains a few traps for unwary singers, however well they may know their notes, for in the first verse both stanzas start with this rhythm —

— but in the second verse we find —

— and just before the first refrain there is an intriguing half-bar overlap between voices and orchestra.

Occasionally, of course, a simple lyric would immediately suggest a melodic rather than a rhythmic outline, but even then Sullivan would carefully weigh the advantages of various alternative time-signatures and perhaps eventually place it in 3/4 (or 9/8) instead of the 2/4 (or 6/8) that could have been expected. Many composers, if setting these words from *Ruddigore* and *The Yeomen of the Guard*, might have written —

— and —

— but Sullivan had the initiative to extend or compress the

obvious time-pattern, and thereby raised the melodies out of a rut of banality.

This was definitely a question of technique rather than inspiration; more than once a 3/4 tune from an opera appears in the overture in 2/4, which may have been its original form.

It was certainly in triple time, especially in slow or moderate *tempi*, that Sullivan found it easiest to achieve rhythmic contrasts. The preamble to 'The world is but a broken toy' (*Princess Ida*), for instance, establishes 3/4 just as the preamble to *Ungeduld* establishes 9/8, yet the opening phrase for the voice, like Schubert's, carries with it a *suggestion* of duple time. This ambiguity is even more marked at the chorus entry 'Acclaim him who, when his true heart' in the first-act finale of *Ruddigore* and in 'We are warriors three' (*Princess Ida*), where aural uncertainty is not dispelled until the last bar of the first verse.

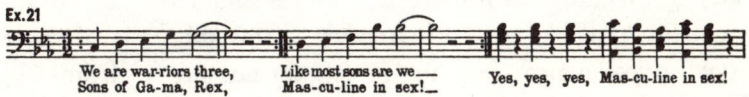

Several of the examples just cited, notably 'Three little maids from school are we', make it clear that Sullivan by no means *depended* on short lines or metrical irregularity to stimulate his inventive power. More formal measures served the purpose equally well, provided that he could escape from strophic restrictions. There is nothing unusual in the metre of 'Long years ago, fourteen maybe' (*Patience*), yet we notice at once the composer's scrupulous attention to detail. The accentuation is cunningly varied during the eight bars allotted to the first stanza; for contrast the second — which also consists of four iambic tetrameters — is squeezed into *five* bars. In the section beginning 'Ah, old, old tale of Cupid's touch' the treatment is yet again different (with a novel form of accompaniment in which bassoon and *pizzicato* basses figure prominently). This is by no means an isolated instance of a stereotyped lyric being brought to life by Sullivan's clever variations on note-values. Look at these few bars from *Iolanthe*; at first glance there is nothing very remarkable about them, but more careful examination will reveal that placing the word 'Tears' on the third beat of a bar — instead of on the first beat of the next bar — gives it just the right emphasis, and incidentally helps to lift the mawkish lines to somewhere near the level of true pathos.

Ex. 22

He loves! If in the by-gone years Thine eyes have e-ver shed Tears— bit-ter un-a-vail-ing tears—For one un-time-ly dead—

It was not only in pastiche — *e.g.* the Slow Dance from *Kenilworth* (see Ex. 2, page 10) and the minuet from *The Sorcerer* (Ex. 161, page 145) — that Sullivan followed the early-eighteenth-century practice of turning two bars of 3/4 time into one bar of 3/2. It often forms the basis of those drawn-out cadences (*e.g.* in 'Hearts do not break' from *The Mikado*) which almost became a mannerism, and it underlies the whole rhythmic pattern of 'Ah, leave me not to pine' from *The Pirates of Penzance*, where in consequence the vocal phrases fall into unequal bar lengths — 3–4–6–4–4.

Ex. 23 Andante

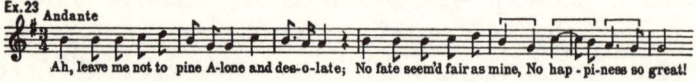

Ah, leave me not to pine A-lone and des-o-late; No fate seem'd fair as mine, No hap-pi-ness so great!

In brisker *tempi*, too, he sometimes used the same device, it later became part of Tchaikovsky's stock-in-trade, but one

should remember that *Di Ballo* —

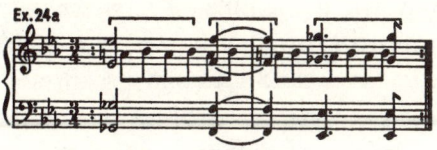

— was written long before *Swan Lake*.

This form of syncopation really derives from that duality of sextuple time which was exploited by Dvořák in the scherzo of his *Symphony in D minor* and later by Sibelius in the second movement of his third, but there is nothing specifically Slavonic or Finno-Ugric about the contrast.   Sullivan took advantage of it to impart artistic verisimilitude to gay *Latin* dance measures, as in *The Gondoliers*, for example.

Once, in *The Beauty Stone*, a strand of linear counterpoint is pulled from the rhythmic texture (see also Ex. 87, page 90) —

— and there is an interesting but not very successful experiment in *Utopia Limited* where the tune of 'O make way for the Wise Men !' is first heard in a rather pompous 3/4 and is afterwards repeated with identical note-values in a jaunty 6/8.

The flair for appropriate verbal accentuation which is such an outstanding feature of Sullivan's best work must not blind us to the fact that his talented craftsmanship in other departments helped to ensure his success. One of his most deservedly popular songs — 'There lived a king, as I've been told' from *The Gondoliers* — is rhythmically unadventurous, yet although it has a tune which the man-in-the-theatre can whistle when he comes out into the street its formal symmetry is perfect and every bar will stand inspection by a trained musician. Never afraid of the obvious, he was sometimes content to set jog-trot jingles to music that was equally jog-trot and perhaps none the worse for that, but even where the words were of primary importance he sometimes pointed them with a deft individual touch. There is an early instance in *The Contrabandista* (libretto by F. C. Burnand); unfortunately the accent on the second beat of the bar that is so suitable for 'strut' becomes a false one when the same notes are forced to fit the second verse.

Ex.27

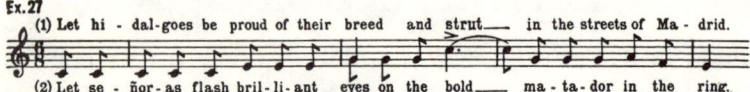

(1) Let hi - dal-goes be proud of their breed and strut___ in the streets of Ma - drid.

(2) Let se - ñor - as flash bril - li - ant eyes on the bold___ ma - ta - dor in the ring.

Once he became accustomed to *Gilbert's* idiosyncrasies, Sullivan found little difficulty in ringing the changes. Essentially there is not much metrical difference between —

(1) 'If you're ánxious for to shíne in the hígh aesthetic líne as a mán of cúlture ráre';

(2) 'When you're ly'ing awáke with a dísmal headáche and repóse is tabóoed by anxíety';

(3) 'When the níght wind hówls in the chímney cówls and the bát in the moónlight flíes'.

Certainly Gilbert had the lilt of *Patience* and *Iolanthe* in his head when writing *Ruddigore*, and he had a shock when he first heard —

Ex. 28

When the night wind howls in the chim-ney cowls and the bat in the moon-light flies, *etc.*

— for he 'had hoped that the scene would have been treated more humorously'.

Even in this superb song, however, Sullivan fell into the old *Contrabandista* trap of allowing a stress that was appropriate in the first verse to do duty again in the second (and third); in such cases judicious editing is advised and, so far as I know, not even those fanatics who regard Sullivan's every note and phrase-mark as sacrosanct have ever complained that —

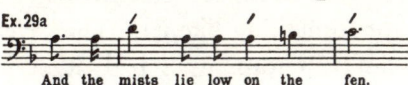

Ex. 29a

And the mists lie low on the fen.

— has for many years been rendered —

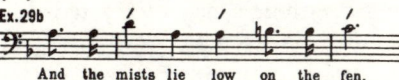

Ex. 29b

And the mists lie low on the fen.

— and so appears in the latest edition of the vocal score.

On the other hand he occasionally introduced an effective contrast when it was most welcome. In Dame Hannah's song from Act I of *Ruddigore* melody and rhythm are alike commonplace, but half-way through the third verse both are dramatically interrupted, and the number is thereby given a touch of much-needed distinction.

Ex. 30

The pro-phe-cy came true: Each heir who held the ti-tle Had, ev-'ry day, to do Some crime of im - port vi-tal; Un-til with guilt o'er-plied "I'll sin no more!" he cried, And on the day he said that say, In a - - go-ny he died!

Sullivan's versatility was amazing; he would turn from doggerel one minute to blank verse the next. In *Kenilworth*, at the age of twenty-two, he had been faced with —

> Look, how the floor of heaven
> Is thick inlaid with patines of bright gold:
> There's not the smallest orb which thou behold'st
> But in his motion like an angel sings,
> Still quiring to the young-eyed cherubins;
> Such harmony is in immortal souls.

Whether or not his tune had caught the spirit of Shakespeare's lines is for the moment neither here nor there; at least he had shown proper appreciation of their underlying rhythm and the experience served him well, for Gilbert wrote many passages in blank verse (or something like it). They were intended for recitative, but Sullivan sometimes had other ideas. Look at the short number 'Now for the pirates' lair!' from Act II of *The Pirates*; every sentence, nay every word, is treated on its merits, and it would be hard to construct a vocal line better fitted to the natural rise and fall of the verbal phrases.

Elsewhere, too, Sullivan showed the same skill in this type of transformation. One should study the long passage marked *allegro doppio movimento* in the first-act finale of *The Yeomen*, and notice the orchestra's part in the conversation.

In *Ivanhoe*, however, blank verse got Sullivan down. Although a layman might feel that Julian Sturgis' libretto, *qua* libretto, received unduly harsh treatment from professional literary critics (Bernard Shaw, for instance, in his dual capacity, overpraised the music but inevitably lampooned the words), there was admittedly an undue proportion of stilted iambic pentameters.

> And thou shalt share my glory and my pride;
> For I will make thee Empress of the East,
> Carve thee a throne more fair than Solyman's —
> And thou and I, fearing nor man nor God,
> Shall sit on high, the crownéd monarchs of the world.

This sort of thing, even if it ended with a needless alexandrine, could not be expected to give a composer much encouragement.

Sullivan did his best to provide an effective climax by extending the last line into a rhapsodical outburst, but he slipped up (unnecessarily) when he stressed the word 'of' in the cadence. He was more successful in the final stanza of 'Woo thou thy snowflake', quoted in Ex. 33 below; it is melodically satisfying, and although the rhythmic treatment is not particularly original it is at all times quite appropriate. The whole of this song, moreover, has a passionate intensity that is unusual for Sullivan.

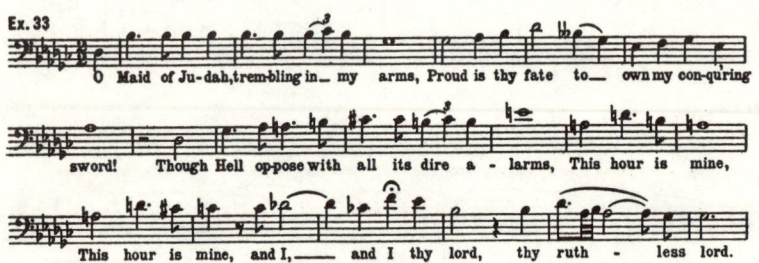

If a lyric did not immediately suggest a satisfactory melodic phrase to his mind, nor on closer investigation stimulate his rhythmic imagination, Sullivan lost interest, and in setting it to music followed the line of least resistance; hence the tedium of his early oratorios. When he lapsed into rigidity or in-apposite accentuation in the operas it may sometimes have been because Gilbert's words failed to inspire him (and indeed they could be extremely trivial), but we must also remember that when pressed for time — as he often was — he tended to dash down the first thing that came into his head. Sometimes he even used ready-made tunes without any regard for either metre or sense, which may account for the astonishing inepti-tude of 'Oh ! happy the lily' (*Ruddigore*) and 'Oh, sweet surprise — oh, dear delight' (*Utopia Limited*). The same excuse will hardly explain away this passage from *The Golden Legend*, where perhaps he was merely being perverse.

In spite of such occasional lapses, Sullivan's reputation deservedly owes much to his extraordinary gift for word-setting. In this chapter we have briefly reviewed his methods of approach; it has not been possible to cite more than a few instances of his almost uncanny skill in making the unexpected accent sound natural and indeed inevitable. This characteristic facility (together with greater resource in modulation) raises his best light music well above the level of Messager's for instance, which in other respects merits comparison. As for his avowed imitators in this country — Lionel Monckton, Edward German, Sidney Jones and so on — they rarely even attempted to follow his lead towards rhythmic variety. Among popular contemporary composers in the same genre only Vivian Ellis has occasionally taken a tentative step in the right direction. If any Sullivan-worshippers think it blasphemy that the name of their idol should be mentioned in the same breath as that of a composer of successful musical comedies, they may care to reflect on the significance of the fact that Ellis has long enjoyed the advantage of collaborating with Sir Alan Herbert, many of whose lyrics are as original, as distinguished and as *metrically irregular* as those of Gilbert himself.

CHAPTER V

HARMONY—A FEW SIGNPOSTS

SULLIVAN'S harmonic resource does not match his rhythmic ingenuity; it often waits on melodic inspiration and rarely shows much initiative, though now and again it lends a helping hand in a tight corner or with a subtle touch points the way round an arid patch of triviality or a slushy puddle of cheap sentiment.

Brought up in the classical tradition, he was soon using the conventional formulae of Auber, Donizetti and Balfe with professional competence and occasionally brought off an unexpected modulation with a panache worthy of Schubert (for an early instance see Ex. 6, page 14). He learnt a few more tricks from Mendelssohn and Schumann, but as time went on became increasingly indebted to Gounod and Bizet. In swift transitions from key to key he sometimes managed to combine the former's smooth technique with a refinement more characteristic of the latter, but in the long run the *savoir-faire* of the two Frenchmen eluded him. He absorbed all that he heard or read, and although contemporary music did not much attract him he was not above taking a few hints from Wagner and Parry when it suited his purpose. At one time it seemed just possible that these diverse elements might be fused into a unity, but the signs were few and soon became far-between; in retrospect they are seen as pan-flashes. In the harmonic field he remained to the end an eclectic; he had easily recognisable *habits* but his *style* never achieved individuality or even homogeneity.

When he first started writing operas Sullivan nearly succumbed to that tonic/dominant tyranny under which Benedict, W. V. Wallace and young Verdi had laboured. When we remember, however, that on some of their less distinguished pages Bellini, Weber, Mozart and even — let's face it — Beethoven had been under similar restraint, we should be ready to overlook those few choruses from *The Sorcerer* and *The Pirates of Penzance* that tend to recall the worst features of *The Lily of Killarney* and *Maritana*. Rather let us note how soon there were signs that Sullivan was freeing himself from these grim fetters. At the climax of their welcome to Sir Joseph Porter and his retinue, the true-blue sailors of H.M.S. Pinafore indulge in chromatics as adventurous as any that lend interest to the second-act finale of *Fra Diavolo*, and while an abrupt modulation from E flat major to G flat major just saves the Austrian March in *The Bohemian Girl* from lapsing into grey monotony, in *Patience* the Soldiers of Our Queen add to their extravert chorus a splash of harmonic colour that is as brilliant as the scarlet of their uniforms.

Even in the frankly comic songs, where the importance of throwing the words into effective relief is almost all that matters, Sullivan rarely follows the path of least resistance. The penultimate line in each verse of the Judge's song from *Trial by Jury*, for instance, is quite deftly harmonised, and 'My name is John Wellington Wells' (*The Sorcerer*) has some realistic touches, especially in the passage beginning 'He can raise you hosts Of ghosts'. The same eerie atmosphere is even more successfully caught in 'When you're lying awake' (*Iolanthe*), though here it is the descriptive orchestration that really arrests our attention.

The two last-named songs, admirable as they both are in their way, also serve to draw notice to one of Sullivan's harmonic weaknesses — his reliance on tonic pedal point. One can tolerate the device in a patter song, and appreciate its legitimate employment as a drone bass (*e.g.* in 'I have a song to sing, O !' from *The Yeomen of the Guard*) or to emphasise the home tonic at the end of a work like the *Di Ballo* overture. But it became such a habit with Sullivan that an objective observer might well adduce lack of enterprise or even down-right laziness. Such a charge is difficult to refute if one refers to only two examples out of many: the opening chorus of Act II, *The Gondoliers*, and the song 'Bold-faced ranger' from *Utopia Limited*. Of course Sullivan was only following the lead of Donizetti (cf. the chorus 'Che scena ! che imbroglio !' from *The Daughter of the Regiment*) and Gounod (the duet 'Nuit d'hyméné' from *Romeo and Juliet*). Indeed he could cite higher authority, for the last movement of Mendelssohn's fourth symphony maintains a tonic bass for its first nineteen bars, but such a brilliant pastiche could be a dangerous precedent for a less resourceful composer. It must be added that Sullivan, when he wanted to, could write a tonic pedal in an *inner* part as well as anyone, witness this passage from *The Mikado*.[1]

Ex. 35

Although Sullivan grew up during the heyday of Mendels-sohn-worship in this country and emulated him in many ways (especially delicacy of orchestration), in the first few operas he

---

[1] The Neapolitan sixth would be more effective had the same chord not been used just previously — and more appropriately — in setting the words ' A dreadful *fate* You'll suffer all the same '.

rarely lapsed into those harmonic clichés which mar some of Mendelssohn's more sentimental effusions. But the duet 'Long years ago, fourteen maybe' (*Patience*), though it has some admirable features which have been discussed in Chapter IV, marks the top of a slippery slope down which Sullivan continued to slither without ever recovering his balance.

This interlude sounds very pretty on the orchestra but the derivation is all too clear, the danger sign is there, and it is no surprise when we reach the vocal cadence.

(In some of the D'Oyly Carte performances between the wars, the *pizzicato* B's in the bass were the sole accompaniment for the word 'lit-tle', and the band-parts were altered accordingly. This was a happy inspiration, for when the right-hand piano chords are omitted the passage certainly sounds less hackneyed. But Sullivan is sacred and the original version has now been restored.)

Hitherto this progression had only occasionally reared its head in an opera — although it did so rather flagrantly at the end of 'Fair moon, to thee I sing' (*Pinafore*) — but thereafter Sullivan worked it to death; that wretched augmented fourth introduced an unwelcome touch of cheap pretension or false pathos into far too many cadences. His addiction to this facile trick has been a boon to his detractors and a source of embarrassment to his defenders. Nearly every composer has his Achilles heel; Sullivan, having recovered from some of the growing pains of his adolescence, developed this new weakness just as he was approaching his prime.

Like many of his contemporaries he often used that notorious chord, the diminished seventh, as an elementary approach to the dominant seventh. In its simplest form this is a mere convention (see the last two chords of Ex. 171 on page 149), but Ernest Newman in his *Opera Nights* quoted two bars from *Les Troyens* 'to illustrate the immense psychological difference between a Berlioz phrase in the colour-medium in which it was conceived and the same phrase in the black-and-white of the piano'.

Ex. 38

The effect also varies greatly according to the context and can hardly be gauged without reference to the character of the music. There are two bars in the finale of *Trial by Jury* which must surely sound blatant to any but the most unsophisticated ear, but one would be squeamish indeed if one's gorge were to rise at the *pizzicato* accompaniment to the chorus of 'In vain to us you plead' (*Iolanthe*) where the actual notes are almost identical. In the hands of a master the formula can become an instrument of deep poetic expression —

Ex. 39

— yet when Sullivan follows Wagner's lead very closely in *The Golden Legend* (Scene 2, at the words 'For at Salerno, far away') we are unaware of any emotional impact whatever. In *Ruddigore*, on the other hand, the same musical idea is very charmingly developed, this time in a mood half humorous, half tender.

The standard progression is intriguingly varied in the lead-in to the first chorus entry at the beginning of Act II, *The Mikado* ; here the diminished seventh chord *drops* to the dominant seventh instead of rising to it.

Soon after audiences were first startled by the cry of 'Barrabam' in the *Matthew Passion*, lesser composers than Bach (and some nearly as great) dropped into the easy habit of using the diminished seventh as a sort of elementary shock-treatment in moments of tension. Sullivan fell heavily, but as this is really a question of dramatic style rather than of harmonic technique it will be discussed in a later chapter.

During Sullivan's lifetime a somewhat uncritical admirer (Charles Willeby) wrote : 'It is frequently under the spell of another that he is most himself. For whoever that other may be — be he Schubert or Mendelssohn, Gounod or Bizet — it is only in the light of Sullivan that he is visible.   And thereby the latter's own individuality is the more prominently thrown up.'   This seems a little obscure, but if the writer means what I think he does there is a grain of truth hidden in the verbiage. Below are four passages, all from Act II of *The Pirates of Penzance*.   If one were to hear them for the first time out of context and were asked to name the composers, one might quite possibly attribute them to Schubert, Mendelssohn, Gounod, Bizet, in that order.   Yet on learning the truth one would kick oneself for not having recognised Sullivan's touch in all four.

(B♭ sustained in bass)

His harmonic vagaries are not always so elusive.   Perhaps he is at his best when he eschews all foreign influence and achieves charming effects by the simplest diatonic means. Here is another phrase, a very familiar one, from the same act of the same opera.

Ex. 43

There could never be any doubt as to who wrote *that*, and it is as English as our wonderful police themselves.

CHAPTER VI

HARMONY—TONALITY AND MODULATION

FOR some reason Sullivan rarely seems altogether at home in the minor. More often than not a piece that starts there will slip into the tonic major (occasionally the relative major) for the last verse or the refrain. This minor/major contrast adds a welcome touch of individuality to some of his early pot-boiling ballads like *County Guy*, but we grow rather weary of it when it is used so regularly in the operas, including even *Ivanhoe*; in 'Lord of our chosen race' each *verse* is in A flat minor although the key-signature throughout is A flat major. (The glorious D major dawn that ends the Lord Chancellor's D minor nightmare in *Iolanthe* comes into a totally different category; this is no mere formality — it is a stroke of genius.)

In the thirteen 'Gilbert-and-Sullivans' (leaving *Thespis* out of account) there are only eighteen numbers — including three more or less self-contained excerpts from first-act finales — that *end* in a minor key, and seven of these are very short pieces of little musical importance. The same tendency is noticeable in his serious works — *The Golden Legend* has only three minor sections (one recurs several times). The long E minor melody from the symphony quoted in Ex. 4 (page 11) strives to establish the *romantic* mood of the first movement of Mendelssohn's violin concerto, but in this mode Sullivan practically never conjures up the *vivacity* of such things as the *Rondo capriccioso*. One possible exception is a number from the forgotten ballet *L'Ile enchantée* (it was afterwards transferred to *The Merry Wives of Windsor*).

Ex. 44 Allegro non troppo e scherzando

Nor does he often use the minor in the forthright manner of Verdi; he nearly always associates it with anxiety, mystery or gloom, and it is significant that in the uninterrupted sunshine of *The Gondoliers* there is only one passage, twenty-two bars long, with a minor key-signature.

Once or twice in the early operas Sullivan exploited the resources of the minor with purely comic intent. The duet 'Oh, agony, rage, despair' from *The Sorcerer* is quite a little *tour de force*, and 'Kind Captain, I've important information' from *Pinafore* is almost as good. But perhaps this came to sound dangerously like self-parody, and the composer felt he had pricked his own skin in a tender spot. In later works the comedians sometimes patter away in the minor, but there is rarely any attempt to realise its potentialities for humorous expression.

A few cases can be cited, however, where the minor is used on its own merits. There is nothing either sinister or sorrowful about the very first number in Sullivan's first completed opera, *Cox and Box*, which is a jolly if rather crude Handelian parody. The duet 'Stay, Frederic, stay' from *The Pirates of Penzance* and the trio 'Of all the young ladies I know' from *Iolanthe* show more originality with a curious insistence on the sharpened sixth. 'If somebody there chanced to be' (*Ruddigore*) is entirely light-hearted and very prettily exploits the characteristics of the minor to mirror the rather conscious artlessness of the words. But it will be noticed that all the items just mentioned end with a refrain in the tonic major except 'Stay, Frederic, stay' which is a mere fragment in a *durchkomponierte* section and closes, if anywhere, on the flat leading-note major.

Indeed, Sullivan wrote only five really satisfying pieces of music wholly in the minor — three of them occur during the course of first-act finales. The impassioned contralto solo 'Oh fool, that fleest My hallow'd joys' (*The Mikado*) and the forceful ensemble 'Go away, madam' (*Iolanthe*) are rare instances of Verdi's influence. In the former the harmonic interest is splendidly maintained, and this scene would not be out of place in *Aida*. The latter is a free variation on a theme that recurs constantly throughout *La forza del destino* and in turn surely derives from the *Egmont* overture. To facilitate comparison with 'Go away, madam', both are here transposed to G minor. (It may be added that Sullivan's subsequent treatment of the phrase is more reminiscent of Beethoven than of Verdi.)

The impressive funeral march from *The Yeomen of the Guard* is even more noteworthy; there is an unexpected modulation to the flat supertonic major and the cadence is particularly original, for a *tierce de Picardie* is used in the $\frac{6}{4}$ that precedes the full close but not in the final chord itself. (By a strange chance the crucial bar does not figure in the autograph score except in a different hand-writing on a narrow slip that still adheres to the original thanks to a small piece of stamp-paper. But the apparent omission of one bar — at the end of a page — was an obvious oversight, and there is no reason to suppose that Sullivan did not write the whole passage himself.) The trio 'We are warriors three' (*Princess Ida*) is in quite a different style; the *staccato* octaves on the strings, which suggest a *basso ostinato* without actually forming one, find effective contrast in the colourful bursts of interruption from brass and wood-wind, and the rousing chorus really stirs the blood.

Lastly, there is Sir Roderic's song 'When the night wind howls' from *Ruddigore*, unquestionably the finest piece of descriptive music that Sullivan ever wrote, worthy of a place beside Schubert's *Erlkönig*, Wagner's overture to *The Flying Dutchman*, and well above Saint-Saëns' *Danse macabre*, all of which are tone-paintings in a similar colour. Although the vocal score gives not a hint of the uncanny brilliance of the orchestration, it demonstrates the sure footholds by which the music in a round dozen bars finds its way from D minor to A flat major and back and the shattering impact of the *fortissimo* chorus entry at an interrupted cadence on the chord of B flat major. The progressions that follow look to be unusual, but if we study them carefully we realise that here Sullivan is not feeling his way in unfamiliar territory. Rather we may find in these few bars an apotheosis of his matured harmonic resource, just as in a few bars at the climax of *Falstaff* (Act II, figure 66) we find an apotheosis of Verdi's.

Apart from such exceptional cases, when Sullivan writes in the minor his modulations tend to follow well-worn tracks to the mediant (the relative major) and the inevitable dominant — when he turns aside to the subdominant minor in 'Sorry her lot who loves too well' (*Pinafore*) it comes as quite a surprise. He is also overfond of a certain short cut to the flat leading-note major (it is even used in Sir Roderic's song) and sometimes takes advantage of the modulation to repeat the opening phrase a whole tone lower. Note the resemblance between the first four bars of 'What means this mirth unseemly?.' (*Iolanthe*, Act I) and the first eight bars of 'Bold, and fierce, and strong' (*Princess Ida*, Act I), which is all the more striking because both passages are in the same key.

In the major, Sullivan's modulations are more varied, and occasionally adventurous. When setting short verses — say two four-line stanzas — he is sometimes content with one simple modulation to the dominant, but he often adds interest to the second stanza by passing through a 'dark' key before returning to the tonic or reaching the dominant for a second time. 'When first my old, old love I knew' (*Trial by Jury*) is an obvious early example and another (from *Pinafore*) can be found in Ex. 11 on page 29. This is one of the favourite shots in Sullivan's locker and it rarely misfires. Only now and again does he proceed in this way to a 'bright' key during the second stanza, but a passage from *Ruddigore* deserves quotation, because it also shows how Sullivan could occasionally bring new life to a threadbare harmonic cliché (*a*).

Generally speaking, Sullivan only modulated to the supertonic minor for the purpose of repeating the opening phrase in that key (*e.g.* the refrain of the lullaby from *Cox and Box*); this was a plausible imitation of his beloved Schubert, but he managed to impart an individual touch to 'When Britain really ruled the waves' from *Iolanthe* (see Ex. 147, page 125). In his later works he often made a similar sequential repetition over a tonic pedal, a poverty-stricken device which was one of the distressing features of his decline — from *The Grand Duke* alone half a dozen instances could be quoted. As a rule he was not at his best in this key-relationship, and only once, so far as I can trace, did it become a corner-stone of the structure. The brilliant exception must be cited — it was 'The Sun whose rays' (*The Mikado*) which, as we have already seen in Chapter IV, is a *locus classicus* of Sullivan's skill in combining melodic charm with rhythmic originality; it is no less remarkable for its harmonic symmetry and subtlety. Even the first modulation to the dominant sounds different from usual; the second stanza starts in the dominant minor (of all unexpected keys) and then *closes,* for practical purposes, on the supertonic minor. The transitions are all splendidly handled; an unhurried succession of muted string chords (crotchets in slow 3/4) forms the background, while an oboe touches up one of the crucial modulations. In the refrain (to which on the second time round flute and clarinet add their unobtrusive decoration) there is an effective and unusually emphatic modulation to the subdominant, and the cadence — where Sullivan so often lets us down — is particularly attractive. This chapter is part of an attempt to assess the composer's technical resources, but the qualities which go to make up a work of art defy analysis; every bar of this song shows the hand of a talented craftsman, but it could only have been conceived by a true artist. It is in fact a little gem.

To his credit Sullivan hardly ever falls into the trap of making an early modulation to the submediant (the relative minor) over an obvious descending bass (*e.g.* C, B, A), though once more *The Grand Duke* can provide an unhappy example — the setting of the significant opening line 'When you find you're a broken-down critter'. He rarely makes an early move to the relative minor at all; when he does so in *The Gondoliers* the words are again appropriate: 'Here is a fix unprecedented ! . . . Never was known a case so hard !' His great standby is the mediant; his melodies so often lead in that direction that one sometimes feels this stock modulation is in danger of becoming a mannerism, though one notes with appreciation how often he takes us to the mediant major rather than the more hackneyed mediant minor. And he never shows his resource to better advantage than when moving on therefrom to the chord of the dominant that nearly always precedes the refrain. The progressions are generally quite conventional, but the effect is often charming and occasionally·impressive; there is no question here of imitating Donizetti, Schubert, Gounod or anyone else — this is characteristic Sullivan. Most of his music is so familiar that it is difficult to examine it objectively, but a student might do worse than compare the various means by which Sullivan, in the following cases, solves that apparently simple harmonic problem — how to move naturally and fluently from the mediant to the dominant.

'Oh, gentlemen, listen I pray' (*Trial by Jury*)
'Oh, better far to live and die' (*The Pirates of Penzance*)
'None shall part us from each other' (*Iolanthe*)
'Comes a train of little ladies' (*The Mikado*)
'There lived a king, as I've been told' (*The Gondoliers*)

Even when Sullivan visits more distant regions he rarely fails to find a smooth way home; his escape back from D flat major to E flat major in 'Were I thy bride' (*The Yeomen*) is quoted in another connection on page 116 (Ex. 133). He faced similar problems in those ensembles where each soloist makes his or her own contribution in a different key, for this original device, which is a unique feature of Sullivan's operas, necessitates a series of contrasted returns to the main dominant. Two good examples are 'Expressive glances' (*Princess Ida*) where the verses are in E major, C sharp minor, C major, and 'Then one of us will be a Queen' (*The Gondoliers*) — F major, D flat major, D minor. An even better one is 'When a wooer goes a-wooing' (*The Yeomen*); the first lead-in to the refrain —

— should be closely compared with the corresponding link at the end of the second verse, which by the way starts in C sharp minor, stresses the figure (*a*) on first violins and closes on A major at the beginning of the first bar of Ex. 47b.

(This expressive quartet is full of subtle harmonic touches. Note, for instance, the restrained chromatic progressions for the wood-wind that form such an appropriate accompaniment to the pathetic words 'Food for fishes Only fitted, Jester wishes He were dead', and the strangely moving effect of a simple chord of C flat major over a tonic D flat pedal in the coda — 'Oh, the doing and undoing.')

Of course it may be argued that facility in modulation should be part and parcel of the working technique of any composer worthy of the name, and admittedly Sullivan's skill in manipulation indicates nothing more than exceptional talent; any possible claim he may have to *greatness* lies elsewhere. Now and again, however, we find a harmonic transition which of itself shows a touch of genius. The F major melody of 'When a merry maiden marries' (*The Gondoliers*) is hardly distinguished; perhaps only the pretty accompaniment with its graceful violin figure saves the opening from banality, and a slightly varied repetition in the dominant does not sound very promising. But Sullivan has a trick up his sleeve. He has often modulated from the tonic to the mediant; now he uses a familiar formula to take us from the dominant to *its* mediant, and we find ourselves in the far-away key of E major. We wonder how he is going to approach the refrain and we lay our money on a slightly crude progression that occurred twice in *The Mikado* ('Young man, despair' and 'Three little maids from school are we'), but now the composer is a step ahead of us. He by-passes the dominant and its seventh altogether and takes us straight back to the tonic; moreover, what would normally be a major operation is carried out so smoothly that it is all over almost before we realise what has happened.

There is another brilliant strategic retreat from an apparently untenable position at the start of *Patience*. Here is the passage just before the rise of the curtain.

It looks like an impasse, but Sullivan knows a way out, a very good one too. He repeats the phrase in D flat, makes a subtle change at the fifth bar, and with Schubertian punctuality is back on the tonic in time for the twenty love-sick maidens to start their doleful ditty. (This little preamble is never heard again, but when the maidens enter with Grosvenor in Act II it will be noticed how cleverly the composer momentarily catches the same drowsy atmosphere by twice introducing a chord of D flat major in the key of E flat major.)

A rather similar situation arises in the opening chorus of *Ruddigore*, but this time Sullivan hardly covers himself with glory. The first few bars pin-point another of his inherent harmonic weaknesses — failure to establish the tonic key at the start of a movement. An E flat major phrase (as vigorous as the other was languorous) modulates *immediately* to the dominant and then exactly repeats itself a whole tone lower, so that very early on he is firmly lodged in the subdominant. This is tricky territory and (unlike Beethoven in the *Prometheus* overture and the first movement of his first symphony) Sullivan only reaches safety after a rather undignified scramble; it is a near thing and one is not surprised that he now finds it necessary to emphasise the key of E flat with a long dominant pedal. Worse is to come, for Zorah's solo in the middle of the same number is a really dreadful affair with no feeling of tonality at all. It starts in A flat major and any little character it may have vanishes like the air out of a pricked balloon when it modulates — or rather collapses — into D flat major — that subdominant again! There is then an abrupt transition to C major, a key right out of context, and the subsequent return to the main dominant (B flat) is handled nearly as clumsily. The slipshod workmanship of these two dozen bars is so uncharacteristic that one cannot help thinking that the section must have been hurriedly rewritten as part of a last-minute alteration, possibly by a hand less sure than Sullivan's own.

In the opening passage of *Ruddigore* just referred to, the repetition of the first phrase a tone lower (after modulating to the dominant) involved consecutive major triads, on B flat and D flat. Sullivan is very fond of these jumps from one common chord to another. Often the move is *up* a minor third (as in the *Ruddigore* instance) or *down* a minor third (as at the end of the first stanza of 'When our gallant Norman foes' from *The Yeomen*). Shifts down a major second are less frequent, but one is made with good dramatic effect at Ko-ko's words ''Tis Nanki-poo !' in the first-act finale of *The Mikado*, and Sullivan sometimes makes the same move in midstream, so to speak. Dunhill has justly praised the Peers' Chorus in Act I of *Iolanthe* as a 'truly magnificent piece of consciously aristocratic music', and of all its 'bold changes of key' none is more brilliantly conceived than that from E flat to D flat for the words 'Paragons of legislation'.

Used with imagination a shift to the flat submediant — that is, down a *major* third — can be impressive (*e.g.* the return to the *tempo primo* after the *più animato* section of the chorus 'Be not afraid' from *Elijah*) or even terrifying (the double-bass entry at the end of the 'Ave Maria' from *Otello*). If Sullivan never emulated Mendelssohn or Verdi, on the other hand he rarely perpetrated such a *gaffe* as the first F major trombone chord in the introduction to *Carmen*. He certainly overworked the device ; it occurs seven times in the first twenty minutes of *The Gondoliers*, where it is used (twice) for discreet harmonic contrast and (three times) to heighten the effect of a *forte* chorus entry — only twice as a facile means of changing tonality. But when it is made to serve this *particular purpose* no less than six times in a single opera (*The Pirates*), the composer is not living up to our expectations. On his day, after all, he was unexcelled in the art of *moving* naturally from key to key. He proved this in the first-act finale of *Patience*, where (at second letter D) a four-bar phrase is heard in succession in four different keys, twice over a dominant pedal and twice over a tonic pedal. No two of the transitions are exactly alike; to locate and analyse the tiny variations in melody and harmony that ensure their smooth accomplishment could be a valuable lesson in the art of composition.

CHAPTER VII

HARMONY—USE OF CHROMATIC IDIOM

ALTHOUGH Sullivan's harmonic horizon was limited he was quite capable of springing a surprise, even in his early days. Here are two bars from the introduction to *Kenilworth* (1864).

The setting of the words 'Heard the dull sea-gull's mournful cry', etc. (*Cox and Box*, 1867) is both original and descriptive, and in the short cantata *On Shore and Sea* (1871) we find this unexpected progression.

Suspensions, accented passing-notes and the like are rarely used except in a purely conventional way; there is an interesting resolution (*a*) in the introduction to Act II of *Princess Ida* —

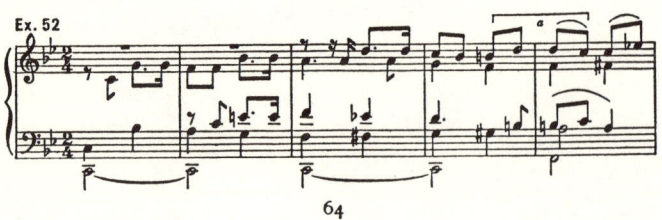

— but this passage from *The Martyr of Antioch* shows a lack of technical assurance.

Ex. 53

More characteristic of the Sullivan we all know are the little dabs of chromatic colour in the link between verse and refrain in 'I cannot tell what this love may be' (*Patience*) and this drawn-out cadence from *Iolanthe*.

Ex. 54

On the other hand the progressions at the end of the beautiful oboe solo in the 'Invocation' from *Iolanthe* and at the words 'For Gama would not dare To make a deadly foe Of Hildebrand' (*Princess Ida*, opening chorus) are obvious importations from across the channel. The following passage (*Patience*, Act I), which might have been lifted straight from *Carmen*, has particular significance —

Ex. 55

— for such simple chromatic transitions, generally pivoting on one note (not necessarily enharmonic of course), were of great value to Sullivan when he consciously and conscientiously tried to widen his outlook in *The Golden Legend* (based on Longfellow's poem). They certainly lend a not unpleasant flavour to Lucifer's glorification of Demon Alcohol in Scene 1, to the second half of Scene 3, and to the climax of Scene 6, which are all so French and yet so very very respectable. This one feels is music such as Massenet might have written for an opera based on *The Rosary* or *East Lynne*. Unfortunately, Sullivan's sincere attempt to make *The Golden Legend* as unlike *The Mikado* as possible resulted in a hotch-potch of harmonic styles. Some of the choruses are in his own worst Moody-and-Sankey tradition. Elsewhere we are reminded of Parry (whose *Prometheus Unbound* had been produced six years before), especially in the short introduction to Scene 1 and in parts of Scene 2, which opens with an exquisite little tone-picture of a quiet summer evening when

> Shafts of sunlight from the west
> Paint the dusky windows red.

For the beginning of Scene 3, however, we go back to Schubert, and the Epilogue (in the course of which one of the themes from Scene 2 is used as a fugal subject) shows Bizet shaking hands with Mendelssohn in a hearty atmosphere of muscular Christianity.

Nor is this all; Sullivan was so determined to show his originality in this *ridotto* that he invited a new harmonic trick which might be called the 'semitone slide'. In Scene 3 (at letter C) he used it with superb effrontery by calmly altering the key-signature from 2 flats to 3 sharps and then proceeding merrily as before, but in the Prologue he lost his head completely and wrote bar after bar of the sort of thing found in Ex. 56. (The 'slide' has been adopted by later composers, Richard Strauss, Delius and Britten among them. Ex. 57 is taken from Act I of *Albert Herring*.)

As the other main ingredients of the Prologue are pealing bells, *tremolando* diminished sevenths, and repetitions in different keys of a meaningless little six-note quaver figure, it is not surprising that one's first impression is one of unsophisticated atonality. Closer study reveals that between letters L and M three fragments of uninspired melody are combined in counterpoint and confirms that the orchestration throughout is worthy of Berlioz.

All this experience served Sullivan well in his next two operas. There is unwonted harmonic richness in the accompaniment to Mad Margaret's song from *Ruddigore*, where in this context the augmented fourth in the cadence for once sounds natural rather than redundant.

Sir Roderic's song has already been discussed (page 55), and while some of the other music in this dramatic scene is only conventionally realistic, the progressions that accompany the line 'Steps into the world once more' are not only unusual, they are positively blood-chilling. At one point in the ghosts' second chorus there is even the suggestion of a whole-tone scale, and the descriptive passage where they return to their picture-frames could hardly have been written two years earlier.

The same remark might perhaps apply to the opening chorus of Act II, *The Yeomen of the Guard*, where there is an impressive modulation to the leading-note major, and certainly to the setting of Jack Point's words in Act I: 'Yet if the fee is promptly paid', etc. Elsie Maynard, too, owes something to her namesake of *The Golden Legend*. Compare 'The night is calm and cloudless' with 'Leonard, my lov'd one, come to me'. Not only are both songs in D flat major with an accompaniment of repeated string chords (quavers in slow 12/8 time); both make an unexpected transition to D major before reaching their climax on a conventional $^6_4$. (Incidentally the florid *melisma* at the end of the latter was evidently an afterthought. The original vocal line was much simpler; the deletion and insertion can be plainly seen in Sullivan's manuscript.)

Another number from *The Yeomen* calls for comment here; the chorus 'Here's a man of jollity'. Perhaps to introduce a touch of sixteenth-century colour, Sullivan sets this in the Lydian mode, which is rigidly maintained throughout. It starts in F Lydian, but when the singers pause for breath on an octave G, the orchestra bursts in *sforzando* and then repeats the whole affair *pianissimo* (during dialogue) in G Lydian. The effect is quaint and rather incongruous. This curious little piece with its strongly modal flavour and frequent changes of time (3/4, 4/4, 5/4) seems to belong more to the world of Vaughan Williams' *Hugh the Drover* than to that of Gilbert and Sullivan's Merryman and his Maid.

Wisely perhaps, the composer eschewed all such things in *The Gondoliers*. Although in Fiametta's first solo 'Two there are for whom, in duty' the ear is caught by two flute passages apparently written for an enigmatic scale, it is soon clear that to evoke an atmosphere of spontaneous gaiety Sullivan has no need to hark back to the sixteenth century or look forward timidly towards the twentieth. Indeed, the only serious criticism that can be made of this opera as a whole is that some of the accompaniments, particularly in the second act, are altogether *too* unadventurous and in fact border on the commonplace; there are few of the chromatic touches found even in a comparatively early work like *Patience*. Exceptionally the duet 'There was a time', in the unusual key of F sharp major, is a noteworthy example of Sullivan's mature style. Here he adapts a favourite Bizet gambit to his own purpose and reaches the flat submediant by direct modulation at the end of the first stanza. It is interesting to compare the two different settings of the second stanza. In the first verse — sung by the baritone — there are two four-bar phrases in D major and the subsequent modulation is rather spoilt by a premature chord of the main dominant in its root position. (On the first beat of the second bar in Ex. 59a a first inversion would have been preferable.)

Ex.59a

In the second verse, however, a more flexible melody for the soprano — with a suitably higher *tessitura* — is compressed into two *three*-bar phrases yet finds time to wander attractively in and out of both G minor and D major, and the approach to the dominant is more skilfully handled (Ex. 59b).

Ex.59b

Although it was too much to expect that a grand opera would rival *The Gondoliers* in uninhibited tunefulness, one might have hoped that by this time Sullivan would have learnt to move with more assurance in that wider harmonic field where he had recently been making tentative explorations. But *Ivanhoe* is almost entirely retrograde. The richer texture for which he was indebted to Parry and which was used so appropriately here and there in *Ruddigore* and *The Yeomen* is discarded in favour of shoddy, and there are few traces of the refinement that graced the emasculated-Massenet scenes from *The Golden Legend* or the mildly Wagnerian atmosphere —

Ex.60

— that was caught now and again in the *Macbeth* overture. Only in parts of the second and third scenes of Act II does the composer use his new-found powers with even fair success.

In his last half-dozen or so operas where his melodic inspiration seems to have almost exhausted itself, Sullivan's harmonic style falls between two stools. He often reverts to the earlier *Pinafore* tradition with little suggestion of Gallic subtlety, but occasionally makes a rather pathetic attempt to revive our flagging interest with a startlingly 'original' modulation. One from G flat major to the enharmonic tonic minor (F sharp) in the duet 'Mother, dearest Mother' from *Haddon Hall* is supportable, but another from *The Rose of Persia* (G major to B flat major in the vocal score, G flat major to A major in the manuscript) sets the teeth on edge. Even the 'semitone slide' is pressed back into service; *Grove* quotes an instance from *Utopia Limited* and here is one from *The Rose of Persia* where both harmony and orchestration are perhaps meant to give added point to the words.

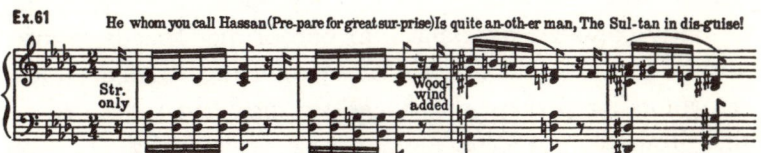

Ex.61   He whom you call Hassan (Pre-pare for great sur-prise)Is quite an-oth-er man, The Sul-tan in dis-guise!

This opera is slightly more worth attention than its immediate predecessors. The duet 'Suppose — I say, suppose', overcoming the handicap of some dreadful baby-talk, may be the best single achievement of this distressing period. The thematic material is simple without being commonplace, and some of the harmonies are interesting. The home tonic is D flat major and there are two contrasted interludes; the first is in G major (!), and though the second starts in the more conventional key of B flat minor it soon finds its way to D major. Except for one rather crude 'slide' of dominant sevenths the unusual progressions are skilfully handled; if Sullivan has here been successful in capturing spontaneity and charm in a comparatively unfamiliar idiom, the good deed is all the more noticeable because it stands almost alone in a naughty world. Here and there, too, he introduces a naïve pseudo-oriental effect by emphasising the flattened seventh; the device is used melodically rather than for harmonic colour and we are inevitably reminded of the Mixolydian mode (perhaps in view of the historical setting it should here be called the Greek Lydian). Far more interesting is a remarkable passage (Ex. 62) which occurs twice during the first-act finale.

Ex. 62

If one listens with eyes closed, is it fanciful to be reminded of
Gerontius tossing restlessly on his bed of pain ? Elgar was only
fifteen years Sullivan's junior, knew him quite well, and
seriously considered making him one of the 'friends pictured
within' to whom the *Enigma Variations* of 1899 were dedicated,
remembering perhaps that the elder man had sponsored the
first production of *Caractacus* at the Leeds Festival the previous
year. One would hardly have expected Sullivan to feel its
impact; might the boot possibly be on the other leg, and
The Dream of Gerontius owe some of its most magical moments
in some slight measure to a few bars from *The Rose of Persia* ? [1]

This was Sullivan's last completed opera; it is terribly
inconsistent. The best numbers show traces of refinement,
even subtlety, that are very welcome after seven or eight years
of almost unrelieved triviality and tedium. It would be
pleasant indeed if one could feel that the composer was at last
dragging himself from the Slough of Despond. Unfortunately
other forces were also at work; now and again, for practically
the first time in the operas, Sullivan descends here to the level
of musical-comedy vulgarity. We prefer to remember *The
Rose of Persia* for those few pages where the novelty of the
harmonic style lets in a breath of fresh air and gives us a fleeting
glimpse of what might have been.

[1] In Act I of *The Emerald Isle* (vocal score, page 107) there is an unusual modulation from E major to F sharp major which also has a whiff of Elgar about it. But
although the passage occurs in one of the numbers sketched out by Sullivan, it was
almost certainly completed and harmonised by German, whose style (in his serious
orchestral works at least) often shows a curious affinity with that of his great
contemporary.

CHAPTER VIII

COUNTERPOINT

MILLAIS rarely painted a nude, Dickens rarely wrote a short story, George Robey rarely acted in Shakespeare, and Hutton rarely made a late cut. When they did so their technique enabled them to get away with it, but in the long run they found such experiments unprofitable; they were not typical manifestations of mastery. Similarly in the world of music: Beethoven never composed a bad opera, Verdi a bad string quartet, Delius a bad piano concerto or Sullivan a bad fugue; but healthy instinct warned them against devoting too much time to what did not come naturally.

Though Sullivan never wrote a *bad* fugue, perhaps only in the Epilogue to *The Golden Legend* did he complete a really satisfying one. Even this hardly accorded with text-book requirements, for he struck unorthodox chords by harmonising the first statement of the subject, but in the passage between the *stretto* and a conventional chorale he showed true musicianship by giving the trombones (*piano, crescendo*) the theme with which the Epilogue opened but which played no part in the fugue itself.

On the other hand these suggestive entries from Act II of *Ivanhoe* —

Ex. 63

— lead to nothing more exciting than some sequential development of the figure marked (*a*), and the gigue from the ballet *Victoria and Merrie England* (1897), which starts so promisingly, soon dissipates interest.

Ex. 64

Another number from the same work is probably Sullivan's second-best fugue.

Ex. 65a

The admirable subject gets the episodic treatment it deserves; only when we expect a *stretto* are we let down by the composer.

Ex. 65b

(This remarkably contrapuntal ballet also contains a two-part invention which is Sullivan's only composition that maintains 5/4 time throughout, unless one counts a short self-contained section from the third-act prelude of his music for *Macbeth*.)

At the time of *The Tempest* (1861), Sullivan was addicted to Schumannesque canons —

Ex. 66

— while at the other end of his life *The Bartered Bride* had a momentary look-in on the ill-fated *Beauty Stone* (1898).

Ex. 67

In *The Merchant of Venice* (1871) one finds passages like this —

Ex. 68

— but in the familiar operas he rarely adopted a fugal style except for poking fun at legal pedantry (*e.g.* the entrances of the Judge in *Trial by Jury* and the Lord Chancellor in *Iolanthe*).[1] His technical resource, however, served him well in *Princess Ida*, which will be discussed in more detail in Chapter XIII. In 'Brightly dawns our wedding day' (*The Mikado*) and 'When the buds are blossoming' (*Ruddigore*), too, the charm of the melodies is greatly heightened by the contrapuntal skill with which they are treated. The former is a particularly happy instance of Sullivan's knack of combining technique with inspiration and thereby pleasing both don and errand boy. The latter, however, is also noteworthy for the contrast obtained by introducing a choral line — first for sopranos, then for tenors — into a vocal quartet. Two other 'fa-la-la' pieces from *Haddon Hall* and *The Rose of Persia* are less effective because the thematic material is poor. In another number from *Haddon Hall* there is an unusually polyphonic passage where the main melody (Rupert's) is almost swamped by the flow of counterpoint (Ex. 69).

[1] Puccini made the same joke in *Gianni Schicchi*.

Most of Sullivan's part-songs, however, have little or no contrapuntal interest and therefore hardly call for mention here; many of them diffuse the odour of a mid-Victorian drawing-room but, thank goodness, he was also at home in a healthier outdoor atmosphere. 'Strange adventure, maiden wedded' (*The Yeomen of the Guard*), for all its four-square rigidity, captures something of the spirit of Dowland's 'Never weather-beaten sail', and a survivor from the unfinished opera *The Sapphire Necklace*, a genuine madrigal for S.S.A.T.B. almost reminiscent of Morley, also shows that Sullivan did not consciously steer himself away from the influence of the sixteenth and early seventeenth centuries. As it is long since out of print, a few bars from this curiosity may be quoted.

Later in his career Sullivan lost caste with some of his high-principled contemporaries because he was adulated in an artistic half-world made up of musical amateurs — who might have had no talent but whose social standing was beyond reproach — and a few struggling professionals who strove to cultivate their acquaintance. (Is the genus extinct even today?) These self-appointed experts were wont to refer to Sullivan as the English Mozart, without quoting a single bar to support their case. It was rather hard luck on Sullivan really, for he knew his Mozart through and through; the latter's influence can often be traced in the *shape* of his melodies and occasionally in the *texture* of his counterpoint. In this respect — but in no other — the middle section of the quintet 'Try we life-long, we can never' (*The Gondoliers*) owes something to 'Wir wandeln durch des Tones Macht' (*The Magic Flute*), and at one moment in *The Sorcerer* the 'imitation' in the voice parts — nothing else — suggests that Sullivan was writing a trio for Donna Aline, Don Alexis and John Leporello Wells. (This number was one of the additions for the 1884 revival.)

Ex. 71

Other instances of counterpoint developing naturally out of vocal — or orchestral — treatment will be cited in the next two chapters. (A rare case of its emergence from a *rhythmic* contrast has already been quoted in Ex. 26, page 37.) We must now turn to a discussion of Sullivan's speciality — the simultaneous presentation of two or more distinct melodies previously heard independently.

He liked to think that he had invented this device, and so far as its use for dramatic contrast is concerned the claim was possibly justified. Purists may point to the ballroom scene from *Don Giovanni*, the quartet from *Rigoletto* and the overture to *Die Meistersinger*. But Mozart's stage orchestras are mere background and the little tunes they play have no special significance; with Verdi it was essentially a matter of characterisation; Wagner's *tour de force* demonstrates unity rather than conflict. The embryo may be found in Philidor's 'stage divertissements' but a more likely prototype is the second (D major) overture to *The Barber of Bagdad*, where first and second subjects are thus skilfully combined in the recapitulation.

Ex. 72

When Sullivan went to Leipzig in September 1858 he was befriended by Liszt; the latter probably took his protégé to the first performance of Cornelius' opera which he directed at Weimar the following December. Although on that occasion the original (B minor) overture was played, Sullivan perhaps retained sufficient interest in the work to make a point of hearing the new overture (written in 1873). If so, his quick ear would have immediately detected the singable character of the themes, although the counterpoint does not recur during the course of the opera itself. Was it a coincidence that this *Barber* received its first British production at the Savoy? It was played there by students from the Royal College of Music in December 1891; this could well have been at Sullivan's suggestion, in which case it might be construed as an appropriate acknowledgment of his indebtedness.[1]

In any case, although Sullivan had made experiments in 'tune-combination' in *Kenilworth* (1864) and *The Contrabandista* (1867), the 'Cornelius-contrast' technique is not found till *The Zoo* (1875), where soprano and tenor go into a huddle at one side of the stage, mezzo-soprano and baritone at the other; first each pair sings separately, afterwards together.

Ex.73

Let me gaze up-on thy face, And I've had four tarts and a cou-ple of pears, I've had three buns that were meant for the bears, Two

lean, and lean— up-on thy breast. bags of nuts in-stead of the apes, Ten bis-cuits of var-ious siz-es and shapes.

In later and greater operas Sullivan's usual plan was to combine two contrasted tunes in a straightforward 'double chorus'. There are excellent examples in the first acts of *H.M.S. Pinafore* (all too short this one), *Patience*, *Ruddigore* (see Ex. 74 for the opening bars) and *The Yeomen of the Guard*.

[1] While on the subject of barbers: surely some of the Gilbert-and-Sullivan patter-songs, like 'My boy, you may take it from me' from *Ruddigore*, owe as much to the Bagdad practitioner's 'Bin Akademiker' as they do to the better-known 'Largo al factotum' of his Seville *confrère* with which they have so often — perhaps not very appositely — been compared.

Unfortunately in *The Sorcerer* and in the first-act finale of *Ivanhoe* the tunes are poor and the contrast is insufficiently pointed; in the second-act finale of *Princess Ida*, the opening chorus of Act III, *Haddon Hall*, and 'Now glory to the god who breaks' from *The Martyr of Antioch*, the contrivance sounds artificial because the material is obviously made to measure.

In *The Pirates of Penzance* (twice), *Iolanthe* (a short passage from the first-act finale that sometimes escapes notice) and *Utopia Limited* (twice), Sullivan varies the procedure by setting *solo* voices against a chorus. In Act I of *The Pirates* the effect is particularly happy; Mabel and Frederic sing their rapture in waltz-time while the other girls chatter away about the weather in 2/4, keeping half an eye open for interesting developments.

In Act II of the same opera the device is exploited (most successfully) for the purposes of broad humour, but the first-act finale from *Utopia Limited* demonstrates only too clearly that contrapuntal fluency will not save concerted music from flaccidity when uninspiring lines are set to uninspired melodies.

(It is interesting to compare this with a rather similar passage written eighteen years earlier — *Trial by Jury*, no. 13, beginning at the 39th bar — which is in every way more satisfactory.)

There is no 'double chorus' in *The Mikado*, but to compensate there is a very ingenious trio in which *three* different tunes are heard first separately and afterwards in conjunction. Although Pish-tush's contribution — in D major — sounds less spontaneous than Pooh-bah's or Ko-ko's — which are in B minor — and the passage is hardly a good example of academic counterpoint, the successive vocal entries are tremendously effective.

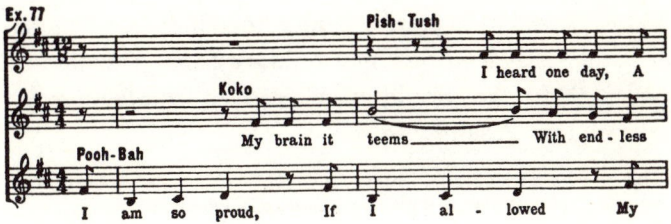

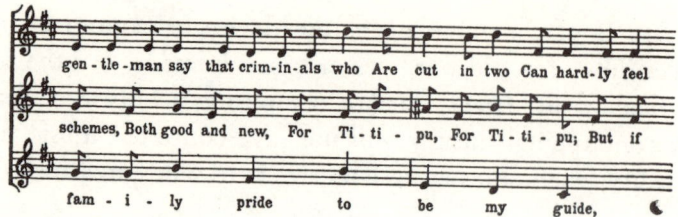

gen-tle-man say that crim-in-als who Are cut in two Can hard-ly feel

schemes, Both good and new, For Ti-ti-pu, For Ti-ti-pu; But if

fam-i-ly pride to be my guide,

One more instance of 'tune-combination' for solo voices remains to be quoted, if only because it adds a momentary flash of interest to the dull background of that depressing opera *The Grand Duke*.[1]

Ex. 78

Julia Per-haps you'll be call-ing When pass-ing this way.— Your bo-gey-dom scorn-ing, And

Ernest To pay— this scorn-ing I give— you warn-ing I'll haunt——

all your love-lorn-ing, I bid you good-morn-ing, I bid you good-day!

—— you each morn-ing, Each night, and each day!—

Outside the operas, Sullivan's addiction to this specialised form of polyphony occasionally led him dangerously near the limits of good taste. He all but slid over them in starting his *Festival Te Deum* (1872) with the first line of 'Oh God, our help in ages past' played on a solo trumpet accompanied by organ (diapason) and then later fitting the same tune most incongruously to the choral words 'Oh Gód, have mércy úpon ús' (*forte*, *sostenuto*) against a jaunty march (*piano*, *staccato*) on a full orchestra helped out by a military band with side-drums and all. (How he would have enjoyed conducting a Cup Final crowd in 'Abide with me'!)

[1] This is a border-line case, because only *one* of the tunes has been heard previously; the same reservation applies to a passage in *Utopia*, Act I, no 8.

As with religion, so with politics. The contrapuntal tendencies of *Victoria and Merrie England* have already been noted, and in this ballet, written to commemorate the Diamond Jubilee of 1897, Sullivan strove to put a musical emphasis on the Unity of Our Islands by combining typical national airs in counterpoint. But the symbolism — or joke if it was one — misfired; England did not come off so badly but Scotland and Ireland were strained beyond endurance, and poor little Wales never had a chance at all.

In fact we are back where we started; paper puzzles were not Sullivan's *métier*. Although he knew the rules as well as any theorist — the tedious fugue 'Oh, that men would therefore praise the Lord' from *The Prodigal Son* might have earned a pat on the back from Ebenezer Prout — he often disregarded them. An astonishing number of his full closes involve consecutive octaves — see for instance Ex. 41 on page 49, Ex. 59a on page 69 and Ex. 86 on page 90 — and flagrant consecutive fifths occur in Ex. 81 (page 85) and Ex. 89 (page 91). Strict counterpoint was indeed far from being his natural mode of expression and we may be thankful that he had sharper, single-edged weapons in his armoury. After all, apart from a handful of academicians and a few rigid adherents to the twelve-note system, nobody really cares whether music is good to look at so long as it is good to listen to. Most of Sullivan's compositions pass this ultimate test with flying colours.

CHAPTER IX

VOCAL WRITING

Sᴜʟʟɪᴠᴀɴ, as we have seen in Chapter II, received his early training at the Chapel Royal; in later life he was on terms of close friendship with many of the great singers of his generation; ballads, anthems, choral works and operas bulk large in his total output. Yet he never realised to the full the unique potentialities of the human voice for musical expression; some of the best songs in his operas are really more orchestral than vocal in character. For instance, 'If we're weak enough to tarry' (*Iolanthe*), charming though it is in its appointed place, only really comes into its own in the overture.

As an ex-chorister, however, he knew 'the value of a kindly chorus' and rejoiced that Gilbert's libretti — unlike those of Italian opera, French *opéra-bouffe* or German *Singspiel* — made it an integral part of the dramatic scheme. Even in those passages where it inevitably occupies a subordinate position musically speaking, its *mezza voce* often provides an appropriate background for the soprano —

— for the tenor (see *Patience*, first-act finale, second letter C), or even for the orchestra (see the funeral march from *The*

Yeomen of the Guard). And sometimes one section — or possibly the whole chorus — takes over the melodic interest even when a galaxy of principals is on the stage. At the end of the long opening number from *The Gondoliers*, for instance, after Gianetta and Tessa have had their say in turn, the sopranos have a verse of their own in 2/4 time against an accompaniment in waltz rhythm by altos, tenors and basses; then comes a joyous moment when the girls in unison revive their flowing introductory melody while the men have a vigorous counter-subject to the same words.

In most operettas (whether composed by Sullivan or any-one else) the last-act finale is merely a straightforward reprise. In *The Gondoliers*, however, two splendid tunes are skilfully dovetailed, and just before the concluding ensemble 'So good-bye cachucha, fandango, bolero', there is a new and thrilling evolution of the bounding phrase from Act I that was quoted in Ex. 25 (page 37). This triumphant paean at the climax of his most characteristic work epitomises all that is best in Sullivan's choral music.

The chorus also plays an exceptionally important part in the first-act finale of *Iolanthe*. Notice —

(1) the clipped rhythm of 'We think we heard him say';
(2) the ingenious accentuation of 'This lady's his *what* ?', given — by a happy stroke — to tenors alone;
(3) the dramatic interjections during Phyllis's solo 'To you I give my heart so rich';
(4) the delicate patter of 'To say she is his mother is an utter bit of folly';
(5) the *fortissimo* climax of 'Go away, madam';
(6) the humour of 'Into Parliament he shall go', sung *forte* and accompanied, and immediately afterwards *pianissimo* and unaccompanied;
(7) the exuberant vitality of 'With Strephon for your foe, no doubt'.

This finale calls for a chorus of some versatility to do justice to all the calculated effects; no details have been scamped by the composer and none should be scamped in performance.

The first-act finale of *The Pirates of Penzance* is a very poor affair by comparison, but at one moment it springs to life. This is when the Pirate King sums up his philosophy in a short solo —

> Although we live by strife
> We're always sorry to begin it:
> For what, we ask, is life
> Without a touch of poetry in it?

— whereupon the whole company bursts into the *fortissimo* unaccompanied chorus 'Hail Poetry! thou heav'n born maid!' The words are a lampoon (Poetry is apostrophised as a Divine Emollient) and dramatically it is indefensible. But coming where it does it is an oasis in a desert of triviality, the choristers at last having something to extend their larynxes, and a full-throated rendering of these seventeen bars has often received a well-deserved encore. Sullivan's share has been decried as a lapse into 'churchiness', and he may or may not have had his tongue in his cheek, but he knew that the audience, steeped like himself in the tradition of English choral singing, would applaud it to the echo. Here, to use modern jargon, he proved himself a 'listener-reaction expert'.

The only other self-contained unaccompanied chorus in the operas is the rather pretentious 'Eagle high in cloudland soaring' (*Utopia Limited*). This is even more reminiscent of the weaker numbers from *The Golden Legend* (especially in its last five bars), but like 'Hail Poetry!' it is quite impressive in its context. These two pieces, however, are all too character-istic of the squareness of Sullivan's choral part-writing, which (leaving aside the formal fugues of his sacred works and the 'double choruses') only shows initiative in spasms. The 3/4 climax of the second-act finale from *Princess Ida*; the fine polyphonic refrain that rounds off each verse of 'When the buds are blossoming' (*Ruddigore*); the concluding section of the opening chorus from Act II of *The Yeomen*; such outbreaks are rare. It is true that the first number of *Trial by Jury* showed a *penchant* for simple choral fugato —

— which cropped up again in *The Martyr of Antioch* in a passage (Ex. 83) that foreshadowed the middle section of 'Comes a train of little ladies' (*The Mikado*).

But in later works Sullivan rarely developed it even to this extent, often failing to maintain interest after a promising start. Sometimes not even the start held out any hope, and in *The Grand Duke* inventiveness touched its nadir.

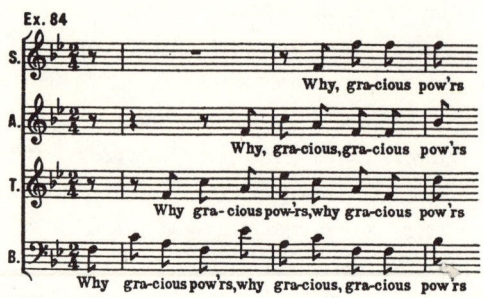

When Sullivan first met Gilbert he was basking in the success of *The Prodigal Son* and he probably did not take *Thespis* very seriously. At all events, in the charming girls' chorus 'Climbing over rocky mountain' he never bothered to write more than a single vocal line, suitable for sopranos. This piece was later transferred *en bloc* from Mount Olympus to the rocky Cornish coast, but the vocal score of *The Pirates of Penzance* leaves it in its elementary form. Editing is required, and in performances the ear detects that here and there the altos sing an octave lower or simple 'seconds'. Unfortunately nothing can be done to correct the faulty lay-out of the opening chorus from *H.M.S. Pinafore*, where the bass part ranges freely from bottom G to top E and the tenor part lies uncomfortably high at the climax.

But these were operatic teething troubles, and as time went on Sullivan began to give more attention to problems of choral *tessitura*. 'Mighty maiden with a mission' from *Princess Ida* and the *Ruddigore* opening chorus (for girls only); the Peers' chorus from Act I of *Iolanthe* and 'In the autumn of our life' from *The Yeomen* (men only); the first-act finales of *Princess*

Ida and *The Mikado* (full chorus) ; these are admirable examples of Sullivan's skill in containing each choral section to its most effective register. Nevertheless, even in the later operas there are a few passages where the part-writing might be — and sometimes is — slightly adjusted in the interests of balance. (One such occurs in the first-act finale of *The Yeomen* at the twelfth bar after letter W.)

In the preceding chapter several contrapuntal passages were cited which serve to draw attention to Sullivan's use of solo voices to add colour to a chorus and vice versa. In many other ensembles — not necessarily involving the chorus — he gives contrasted character to two or more independent voice parts. All his stage-works provide at least one example of a *legato* melody for soprano, tenor, or both, over a subsidiary vocal line composed mainly of repeated notes or simple rhythmic figures. This derives from a conventional formula of Italian opera (cf. the quartet and chorus beginning at figure 22 in Act I of Rossini's *La Cenerentola*) but Sullivan developed it to a fine art. I shall choose for quotation a passage from *The Yeomen* because these few bars demonstrate to perfection his economical workmanship ; not a note is wasted or misplaced and the effect is wholly satisfying.

In the duet 'Welcome joy ! adieu to sadness !' (*The Sorcerer*) he achieved by the same means a *dramatic* contrast almost equal to that of a 'double chorus' ; in the first-act finale of *Pinafore* he varied the treatment so as to emphasise his clever delineation of Dick Deadeye's character (Ex. 86).

Ex. 86

Josephine
Hebe
Ralph

The sky is all a blaze.

Dick
Deadeye

Ex-treme-ly down up-on the wick-ed men, will be ex-treme-ly down up-on the men in man-y var-ious ways.

Haddon Hall cannot often be cited with approval, but the elopement scene contains some good music; in particular there is a charming ensemble where at one moment the soprano strikes out a line of her own over the delicate *staccato* of the mezzo-soprano, tenor and baritone.

Ex. 87

S.
A.

Now, step light - ly, Hold me tight - ly, Creep a long by yon - der

Fare thee

T.
B.

well! Home of my girl - hood, so hap - py, fare - well—

wall! Hush, step light - ly! Hold me tight - ly Where the deep est sha - dows fall.

Interest is far more consistently maintained in the brilliant quartet 'In a contemplative fashion' from *The Gondoliers*; each participant makes a separate contribution to the discussion (*forte*) while the others repeat a *sostenuto* melody (*pianissimo*).

Ex. 88

Tessa

I no doubt Giu - sep - pe wed - ded—That's of

Gianetta
Marco
Giuseppe

In a con - tem - pla - tive

course a slice of luck. He is rath-er dun-der-head-ed, Still dis-tinct-ly he's a duck.

fash - ion, And a tran - quil frame of mind,

Presently the independent entries increase in urgency and at the climax all four singers join in the fray and lose their tempers; the string players in the orchestra — faced with a *pizzicato strepitoso* — nearly do likewise. The whole number is a masterpiece of musical humour.

The ever-popular gavotte that follows soon afterwards also has some clever touches in the voice parts —

— and the quintet 'Here is a fix unprecedented !' (though the part-writing is quite formal) is an even more sparkling affair. In construction it far surpasses its predecessors in *Patience* and *Princess Ida*; on a small scale it is as fine an achievement as the superb example from Act II of *Carmen*, of which it must surely be either an unconscious imitation or a deliberate parody.

In some of the less elaborate ensembles a good effect is obtained when one of the lower parts rises momentarily into unexpected prominence, as in 'Here's a how-de-do' (*The Mikado*) —

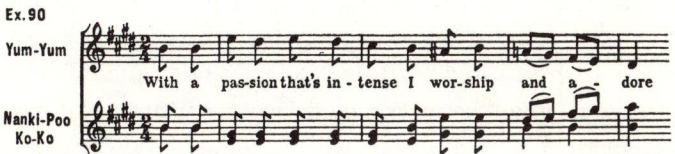

— and in duets the two participants often have imitative or interlinked phrases for a few bars before they join in harmony for the cadence. This is a simple routine to which Sullivan sometimes adds an individual touch. Good examples are:

'Kind Captain, I've important information' (*Pinafore*, baritone and bass);

'None shall part us from each other' (*Iolanthe*, soprano and baritone);

'There grew a little flower' (*Ruddigore*, contralto and baritone);

'Oh rapture ! when alone together' (*The Gondoliers*, soprano and baritone);

'Words of love too loudly spoken' (*Utopia Limited*, soprano and tenor).

Surely it must be as pleasurable to sing these refrains as it is to listen to them.

But Sullivan was not always kind to his soloists. So far as the operas were concerned they were rarely chosen for vocal capabilities alone, yet the range of Pish-tush's big song from Act I of *The Mikado* is:

This may not be an unreasonable stretch for a bass-baritone, but both extremes are used freely, and so that Pish-tush is taking the *top* line in a male-voice trio where his part is written in the treble clef and winds up with *six consecutive bars* on D♯ and E near the top of the stave. Later (at the end of 'Brightly dawns our wedding day') he plumbs bottom F, a note which in some revivals has necessitated the introduction of an apocryphal character called Go-to. Other baritone parts show an almost equal disregard for *tessitura*, and their notation hovers disconcertingly between bass and treble clefs.

Some of the soprano parts, too, are very inconsistent. Mabel in *The Pirates*, for instance, *must* be a coloratura because of 'Poor wand'ring one !', yet 'Dear father, why leave your bed' demands steady beauty of tone throughout the octave F to F, and 'Ah, leave me not to pine' goes a third lower still. Phyllis in *Iolanthe* has an easier time on the whole; most of her part lies in a lyric soprano's best register, never going above G except for one A in the first-act finale, but she is very poorly treated in her first solo which goes down to A below the stave and only once up to D. Here she would be much happier singing a third or even a fourth higher. Nowadays a few self-contained songs or duets for soprano and baritone are transposed, but this solution of the problem is not always satisfactory and often quite impracticable. Nevertheless, in the latest editions of the vocal scores a few such numbers appear in keys different from the original.

That the soubrette parts sometimes have a wide range of two octaves or so is of less consequence; an actress with a pleasant musical-comedy voice can get away with them if she has an attractive appearance and personality. From a singer's point of view the contralto parts are probably the most rewarding, but they all conform to one type and call for that *rara avis*, a real contralto; the stock mezzo-soprano of grand opera is quite unsuitable.

One feels that Gilbert and Sullivan in their corporate capacity did not have much time for tenors. Most of the tenor characters have to be content with but one song (in *Ruddigore* a piece of slapstick at that !) and the poor Duke in *Patience* is fobbed off with a short solo in the middle of the first-act finale. In *Utopia Limited* the whole tribe is guyed, and — crowning insult of all — one of the best tenor songs Sullivan ever wrote — 'Would you know the kind of maid' from *Princess Ida* — is allotted not to the 'leading man' but to his 'stooge'. Nevertheless, the collaborators showed more tenderness for the *amour-propre* of their tenors than that of their sopranos. Most of the conventional Victorian ballads in the operas fall to them (to say nothing of 'Take a pair of sparkling eyes') and these are still a safe passport to popularity.

Rather surprisingly Sullivan only once — in the tiny part of the Boatswain's Mate in *Pinafore* — exploited the simple humour of the lowest register of the human voice. Although one would not have looked for an Osmin or an Ochs even a Don Basilio would have made a nice change, but evidently *bassi profundi* were at a premium during the eighteen-eighties.

Few singers — sopranos especially — regard Sullivan's music with much favour. The reason is not far to seek : his melodies are often Mozartian in character but rarely, if ever, Mozartian in content. Conscientious artists realise that 'Sorry her lot' (*Pinafore*) is as difficult to sing really well as 'Ach, ich fühl's' (*The Magic Flute*), and they ask themselves — frankly is it worth the trouble ? And perhaps one of Sullivan's most valuable technical assets has had a boomerang effect in this quarter ; for most of us the great charm of 'If somebody there chanced to be' (*Ruddigore*) is the appropriateness of the word-setting, but that very feature makes it useless as an audition-piece for which otherwise it would have been well suited.

In this department Sullivan's strength lies in ensemble work rather than solos, but one can compile a short list of songs which give a competent executant plenty of opportunity for expressive vocalisation in a suitable register. If they are not all artistically impeccable, not one of them touches the depths.

Dramatic soprano	Eb–C	'A simple sailor, lowly born' (*Pinafore*) ;
Light soprano	F#–B	'Oh, happy young heart' (*The Sorcerer*) ;
Contralto	Bb–F	'Hearts do not break' (*The Mikado*) ;
Tenor	G–Bb	'Oh, is there not one maiden breast' (*The Pirates*) ;
High baritone	D–A	'Fair moon, to thee I sing' (*Pinafore*).

Other baritones might do far worse than choose that old war-horse 'Time was when love and I were well acquainted' (*The Sorcerer*), which — whether or not taken seriously — is a ballad of considerable distinction.

Even in Sullivan's oratorios and cantatas one notices the same curious detachment where the human voice is concerned. There are no great demands on technique or virtuosity — *bel canto* and gymnastics are alike eschewed — but neither is there much that encourages a singer to give of his best. Santley, Edward Lloyd, Albani and Ben Davies took all this in their stride and never worried the composer with niggling questions about compass or *tessitura*, but they might have been forgiven for doubting whether their talents were being displayed to fullest advantage. Small wonder then that Sullivan, while he was always glad to let unknown and inexperienced artists have a chance to make their name at the Savoy, did not go out of his way to write them parts that would enable them to do themselves justice. His main concern was not the singer, but the song.

CHAPTER X

ORCHESTRATION

ALTHOUGH Sullivan may not be a popular figure with vocalists, by the same tokens those who scrape and blow nearly always enjoy playing his music.[1] He was himself a competent performer on at least four instruments (flute, clarinet, trumpet and trombone) and from childhood he knew and loved them all. For balance and texture he chose the best possible model — Mozart — and the result is visible in the refinement and clarity of nearly all his orchestral scores. His writing for wood-wind soon acquired a delicacy worthy of Mendelssohn, and up to a point he kept abreast of technical developments; his later works have a glitter not found in *H.M.S. Pinafore*, for example. This is a redeeming feature of his last period, for operas like *The Chieftain* and *The Beauty Stone* have little else to recommend them. He even made a few successful experiments which proved that he had studied Berlioz to good purpose.

At the climax of the *In Memoriam* overture and in the *Festival Te Deum* Sullivan allowed his discretion to be overborne by the sheer weight of the forces available,

[1] That fine musician the late Leslie Heward once described to me how during his student days at the Royal Manchester College of Music (about 1914) he was given private object lessons by the leading wind-players of the Hallé Orchestra. He expected them to demonstrate the characteristics of their respective instruments — and their own prowess — in the classic solos from *Euryanthe, A Midsummer Night's Dream, Tristan, Don Juan* and so on, but to his surprise a majority chose passages from *The Golden Legend*. It is pleasant to be reminded that Sullivan's attributes were still appreciated by instrumentalists at a time when his reputation as a whole was under somewhat of a cloud so far as responsible musical circles were concerned.

but as a rule he was very restrained in his use of the full orchestra, and his experience in the theatre soon made him an adept at using limited resources to best advantage. Only fourteen instruments are needed for the first statement of the 'tower motif' in *The Yeomen of the Guard*, but the component parts are so skilfully laid out that the whole is as sonorous as though the band were of Wagnerian proportions.

The overture to *Iolanthe*, too, is a masterpiece of economy; the first brass entry is at the 66th bar — lasting just long enough to give a touch of colour — and the first *tutti* does not occur until the 143rd. At a casual glance the striking *fortissimo* preamble to 'Refrain, audacious tar' (*Pinafore*) seems to call for cornets and trombones to make its effect, yet Sullivan manages all right without either. Again, the wedding chorus from *The Gondoliers* is so well balanced that the accompaniment needs only strings, bassoons and horns; the upper wood-wind is thus left free to support the voices. Generally, however, flutes, clarinets, bassoons and horns in groups perform this duty in choral numbers. The device is often effective, but one is inclined to wonder whether he would have used it so freely if he had been able to place full reliance on the intonation of his singers. On the other hand one can praise almost without reserve his trick of doubling *snatches* of sung melody with wood-wind. I quote the accompaniment to the third verse of

'Expressive glances' (*Princess Ida*), not because it is a distinguished passage (it isn't) but because it illustrates this typical use of clarinets, oboe and flute within a few bars, and also introduces a little piece of counterpoint for bassoon which does not figure in the published score.

As time went on he added these colourful touches with more subtlety, particularly in *The Gondoliers* (of the familiar operas). The duet 'We're called *gondolieri*' is a model in this as in nearly every other respect, but an adequate quotation would take up far too much space. Instead the reader may like to refer to Ex. 171 (page 149) from *The Chieftain*, where the first two-bar phrase is for soprano with bassoon an octave lower, the second for baritone with oboe an octave higher, and both voice parts are thereafter supported by first violins and (momentarily) by two clarinets in octaves. In many of the patter-songs, on the other hand, which are often spoken to music rather than sung, Sullivan made a point of letting the first violins play the tune throughout; perhaps he was afraid that otherwise it might be lost altogether.

Traces of Berlioz' influence first appear as early as the *Marmion* overture (1867).

Apart from a few descriptive passages for wood-wind (*e.g.* in the second verse of 'My master is punctual always in business' from *Cox and Box* and in the 'Incantation' from *The Sorcerer*), fifteen years elapsed before Sullivan ventured to try out Berlioz' technique in the theatre; *Iolanthe* gave him his chance. The vocal score gives a very good idea of the orchestral accompaniment to the first two verses of 'When you're lying awake', but then it loses all touch with reality.

The violins, still in 6/8, gradually become more chromatically minded, while the 2/4 ejaculations of flute and clarinet drop 'off the beat', increase in frequency and eventually spread to the whole wood-wind section. From letter O to the end of the nightmare the excitement is intense and a thoroughly good time is had by all (except the exhausted Lord Chancellor up on the stage).

In his next opera, *Princess Ida*, Sullivan indulged in some more flights of fancy.

Not until *The Golden Legend* did his talent for descriptive orchestration have full fling, however; the Prologue (whatever its other shortcomings) is brilliant in this respect. In *Ruddigore* he showed the same mastery in miniature; as a piece designed to be played by a small band 'When the night wind howls' is still a model. The basic scoring, which remains the same for each verse, must be constantly borne in mind when examining the later decorations. Violins in four parts maintain an eerie shimmering, while *pizzicato* violas at first support the voice and then drop down to pick out an independent bass. Here they are joined, now and again, by a *pizzicato* double-bass playing the same note *in actual sounds*, so that in one bar we have a vertical curiosity (Ex. 96). Tension rises with the magnificent chorus entry, our expectations are

roused, and sure enough once we reach the second verse the fun grows fast and furious against the same background. First 'the sob of the breeze sweeps over the trees' —

— and presently there are scampering semi-quavers on piccolo and top-register flute as 'Away they go, with a mop and a mow, to the revel that ends too soon'. In the third verse 'each ghost —

Superior persons may turn up their noses at such things but they cannot ignore the technical resource that makes them possible. If Sullivan's effects come off every time, it is due to his detailed knowledge of every instrument in the orchestra.

His flute parts are more remarkable for restraint than brilliance. The leader gets an occasional grateful solo like this one from *Patience* —

— and of course has a field day on Mad Margaret's first entrance in *Ruddigore*, but generally he and his partner hunt in couples. There are ten bars near the beginning of the first-act finale from *Patience* where the composer cleverly achieves an 'archaic' effect by leaving a big gap between two solo flutes and a skeleton accompaniment of violas and cellos, and there is an appropriative allusion to 'pipes and tabors' in *Iolanthe* (no. 8, letter G).

But more often than not the simple two-part harmony of the flutes is doubled in the lower octave by clarinets; perhaps Sullivan overworks the device, but in nine cases out of ten the result is so charming that criticism is disarmed. And it was not only in the employment of orchestral resources for descriptive effect that he learnt something from Berlioz; in scene 2 of *The Golden Legend*, for instance, an unaccompanied trio for the soprano and two flutes lasts for eighteen bars.

He made free use of the flute's lower register and at least twice — in 'I'm called Little Buttercup' (*Pinafore*) and 'I cannot tell what this love may be' (*Patience*) — took it down to middle C in solo passages.

Except for an occasional humorous touch ('he whistled an air, did he') Sullivan as a rule used the piccolo only to add brilliance to the flute part — as in the intermission of 'Kind Captain, I've important information' (*Pinafore*) — but it effectively points the violins' arpeggio figuration in the second, fourth, fifth and sixth bars of the preamble to 'Comes a train of little ladies' (*The Mikado*) and at the start of Scene 6 from *The Golden Legend* the instrument is endowed with something like dignity on the independent top line of an elaborate wood-wind ensemble.

Ex.102 Andante tranquillo

Many pundits maintain that an oboe is unsuitable for long solo passages, and certainly most late-nineteenth-century composers followed Wagner's lead and used it mainly for *short* passages requiring great expression. The second movement of Tchaikovsky's fourth symphony was a notable exception and the second movement of Brahms' violin concerto a glorious one, but Sullivan once at least went too far along the same road. Here is the connecting link between the second and third movements of his *Symphony in E*; nothing else happens except an occasional *pizzicato* string chord, and these sixteen bars lead straight to *another* long oboe solo.

Ex.103 Allegretto

After repeating the process (on a smaller scale) in the overture to *The Pirates of Penzance*, Sullivan probably realised that this was too much of a good thing, but the oboe always remained his blue-eyed boy, both on the concert platform and in the orchestral pit. Little snatches of melody admirably suited to its tone-colour seemed to spring naturally to his mind, *e.g.* the *obbligato* in the opening chorus of *Patience* —

— and this 'answer' in *Ruddigore*.

He gave the oboe plenty to do besides playing pretty tunes. One could cite a dozen cases of a *sostenuto* 'binding' a *staccato* or of a single note touching up a string passage that might otherwise sound too subdued. A good example is the A above the stave (not shown in the published piano arrangement) that is held for seven and a half bars from letter H in the *Iolanthe* overture. (See, too, Ex. 95 on page 100.)

The first few bars of Ex. 103 (page 103) show that Sullivan had no text-book inhibitions about the oboe's bottom register, and at the other end of the scale he wrote up to top F, but there is rarely anything to strain the technique of a reasonably competent player. Perfect execution of the descriptive allusion to head-nodding and hand-kissing in 'The criminal cried'

(*The Mikado*) at a steady *allegro comodo* is, however, sometimes beyond the powers of a theatre oboist.

Although Sullivan rarely had an opportunity to write for the cor anglais, he gave it a good outing in *The Golden Legend*; in Scene 2 (between letters S and T) it sings an unaccompanied duet with the soprano that lasts for seventeen bars.

Sullivan fully understood the versatility of the clarinet (one remembers that his father had been a professional clarinettist). He gave it a solo in *L'Ile enchantée* which pleased him so much that when he re-scored the number for *Macbeth* a quarter of a century later he left this passage untouched.

In the operas he allowed it to display its flexibility in the florid cadenza in the first-act finale of *Patience*, its wistful charm in the little solo that precedes 'The world is but a broken toy' (*Princess Ida*), and the more bizarre characteristics of the chalumeau in 'I once was a very abandoned person' (*Ruddigore*). The two clarinets are here quite unaccompanied.

The *legato* thirds and sixths that persist from letter H to letter L in 'When you're lying awake' (*Iolanthe*), the arpeggios in 'The Sun whose rays' and the imitative scale passages (which might so easily have been incorporated in the vocal score) from 'As some day it may happen' (*The Mikado*) —

Ex.109

— these show the same appreciation of the instrument's capabilities and are no whit less effective because they form part of the background. One is sometimes inclined to feel, however, that Sullivan's clarinets hardly have their fair share of the limelight, for although they do splendid work in the frequent 'wood-wind only' ensembles — *e.g.* the introduction to 'Brightly dawns our wedding day' (*The Mikado*), which is scored for oboe, two clarinets and bassoon — they often have to be content with doubling the flutes an octave lower or the bassoon an octave higher. But it must be remembered that Sullivan was writing for a small theatre orchestra, where the clarinets were invaluable maids-of-all-work, ready at any time to play a part that might otherwise have been given to first bassoon, second oboe, third flute or fourth horn.

When the key-signature was appropriate — as in the *In Memoriam* overture — Sullivan had a disconcerting habit of writing for clarinets *in* C. The band-parts have long since been copied out a major second or minor third higher, but occasional difficulties still arise; on a transposing instrument the top G in the opening chorus of *Iolanthe* (at the third bar after letter D) is only just practicable and anyway sounds

shrill. In *The Golden Legend* he went astray by including another virtually obsolete affair — the bass-clarinet *in A*; moreover, he took it down to its bottom note (E sounding C#),
which is theoretically outside the range of the standard bass-
clarinet in Bb, although nowadays some are fitted with an
extension. In *Ivanhoe* Sullivan used the Bb instrument throughout, and gave it a counter-subject that adds a little interest
to the otherwise dull baritone solo 'Forgive, fair maid, the
votaries of the sun'.

Sullivan's orchestral economy can be well illustrated by one
example each of his use of flutes, oboes and clarinets (*a*) in
association, (*b*) in contrast. To these few bars from the prelude
to the fourth act of *The Tempest* the only other contribution
is a featherweight string *pizzicato* —

— and reference to the vocal score will enable the reader to
appreciate the effect of the four tiny solos that decorate the
simple string accompaniment to 'The nightingale Sighed for
the moon's bright ray' (*Pinafore*).

Sir Donald Tovey wrote of a passage in Beethoven's
eighth symphony that it was 'parent of all the bassoon jokes in
the Sullivan operas'. Possibly he was thinking of the policemen's entrance in *The Pirates of Penzance*, but one suspects that

he did not know his Sullivan as well as he might have done, for no composer was more fastidious in his avoidance of orchestral clowning. There is plenty of subtle humour (by no means confined to the bassoon), but there are very few 'jokes' in Tovey's sense. Six notes from *The Sorcerer* might qualify —

— and so would a feeble imitation of a 'clerk scratching a blot' in *Ruddigore*. A few bars after this indiscretion, however, there is a little phrase that is far more typical of Sullivan's sensitive treatment of this expressive instrument.

Indeed the bassoon came second only to the oboe in his affections and the operas are full of characteristic solos like this one (from *Princess Ida*).

Sullivan's early operas require only one bassoon, but from *The Yeomen* onward he used two; one would be sorry to have missed their cheeky chuckles in *The Gondoliers*.

He took full advantage of the instrument's wide compass; bottom B♭'s abound, and here is an exposed passage in the *top* register from his *Symphony in E*.

Ex.117

On the few occasions when Sullivan wrote for a double-bassoon it was only to add depth to the wood-wind bass; he never let it take over the rôle of sorcerer's apprentice. A well-known instance of his frequent use of clarinet and bassoon in octaves is the *Mikado* quotation from Bach's fugue in G minor for organ, but these few bars from *The Merchant of Venice* are more typical.

Ex.118 Vlns.I(doubled by Fl. & Picc.)

Sullivan put all his horn parts in the key of C, as if expecting them to be played on 'natural' horns equipped with 'crooks'; he even wrote for horns *in* D♭, a crook that had never been used and perhaps never existed. A glance at Ex. 93 (page 99) will make it clear that he knew modern valve-horns would be used, for not one of the four parts could be played on the old-fashioned instrument. In his irritating adherence to this convention he was no more blameworthy than many of his contemporaries; indeed the system of notation was defended by Richard Strauss in his commentary on Berlioz' treatise on orchestration. Far more serious is the fact that where the horn was concerned Sullivan took little account of current developments in executant technique and on ninety-nine pages out of a hundred treated it as mere filler-in or 'binder'. In his use of the wood-wind he could challenge anyone — not even such masters of their craft as Wagner, Dvořák, Elgar and Holst have better understood the characteristics of oboe and bassoon —

but apparently he had no such instinctive feeling for the horn. One would have expected him to be influenced in this respect by Mendelssohn and Bizet, but one searches his works in vain for a parallel to the horn solo in the nocturne from *A Mid-summer Night's Dream* or the passage for four horns that precedes 'Je dis que rien ne m'épouvante' from *Carmen*. The nearest approach, perhaps, is in the incidental music for *The Merry Wives of Windsor*. (This canonical duet had previously been heard in *L'Ile enchantée* where it was played in a different key by cor anglais and clarinet.)

A romantic atmosphere is momentarily caught, too, in the overture to *The Yeomen of the Guard*, but here the horn loses something by being doubled in the upper octave by flute and clarinet.

Although now and again, notably in the ensemble at the end of the first scene of *Ivanhoe* and in an entr'acte from *Macbeth* —

— Sullivan exploited that back-and-forth wobble on two notes which Tchaikovsky used to such effect in *Romeo and Juliet* and Brahms in the first movement of his second symphony, his horn parts as a rule read as though they might have been written by a competent eighteenth-century composer — Grétry, for instance — who had suddenly discovered the valve horn and was therefore no longer restricted to the harmonic series.

Some critics have complained because in his light music Sullivan wrote for cornets rather than trumpets. (In *The Contrabandista* he used a bass saxhorn instead of a trombone.) Admittedly the cornet solos in the otherwise refined music for *The Merchant of Venice* (1871) and *Henry VIII* (1877) hold no charm for a sophisticated listener. But in the operas (outside one or two of the early overtures) cornets are used with prudence. Except for an occasional fanfare they are given very few solos in the bad old sense, and even in *tutti* passages they are usually confined to their discreet middle register. Nevertheless Sullivan, like Bizet, knew their value; here are a few bars from the introduction to Act II of *The Chieftain*.

Far better known are the tremendously effective *obbligato* in 'Young man, despair' (*The Mikado*), and the simple rhythmic figure maintained throughout the cachucha refrain from *The Gondoliers*. On the whole one regrets the present-day tendency to replace cornets in Sullivan's theatre orchestra with trumpets, for the larger instruments are too obtrusive in such characteristic passages.

When Sullivan did write for proper trumpets he adopted the same notation as for horns, with frequent changes of crook, so that one is not always sure whether the parts were meant to be played on long-bore trumpets in F (possibly Eb) or on the smaller instruments in C, Bb or A. That he knew his Wagner is clear from *Ivanhoe*, Act II, Scene 3.

He showed more imagination in his use of trombones ; now and again he was almost *too* enterprising. In Scene 3 of *The Golden Legend* the bass trombone has this sort of thing for bars on end.

One notices here Sullivan's detailed instrumental knowledge; the part *as it stands* presents no technical difficulties, but if it had been written in the key of E major or F major instead of G flat major, the figure (*a*) would have required such rapid changes of slide-position as to be practically unplayable. Nevertheless one would hardly hold this passage up as a pattern, and fortunately it can be recorded that though he rarely used the trombones for solo purposes, when he did so he generally treated them with a proper appreciation of their majesty — *e.g.* in the development section of the *In Memoriam* overture (where they are joined by an ophicleide instead of the usual tuba), in *Marmion* (Ex. 93, page 99), in the Epilogue to *The Golden Legend* (see page 73) and in the second-act finale of *The Gondoliers* (the entry is at the twelfth bar after the change of key to C major).

He often gave the heavy department a chance to show that it was as capable as any other of quiet expression. The eleven opening bars of 'To thy fraternal care' from *The Yeomen* are scored for two cornets, three trombones and *pizzicato* double-bass, while brass alone is used for ten consecutive bars in the accompaniment to 'I built upon a rock' (*Princess Ida*). Not until the second stanza are alternate bars given to the strings, a most happy contrast.

Sullivan's string writing is always meticulous, with great attention to detail, but does not always show quite the same distinction that characterises his treatment of the wood-wind. In moments of excitement the violins often have to be content with rushing scales, though now and again they have vigorous bow-work across the strings (see Ex. 56, page 67). The introduction to *The Tempest* includes a remarkable unaccompanied passage in very different vein; this was a rhapsodical flight which Sullivan never transcended. (It leads immediately to Ex. 1 — see page 8.)

The violins are given a delightful scamper in the refrain of 'If you're anxious for to shine' (*Patience*) and here and there in *Haddon Hall* do their best to relieve the tedium —

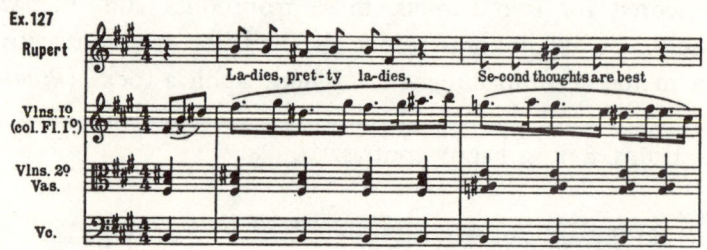

— but in most of the operas there are only occasional bursts of frivolity —

— and one would have welcomed a few more touches of delicate ornamentation like those that adorn a waltz-song from *Utopia Limited*.

Indeed, only in *The Yeomen* is there much violin 'decoration'. Here one notes the sudden flurry at the end of each line in 'Though tear and long-drawn sigh', the unpublished figuration that accompanies Meryll's solo 'Ye Tower warders, nursed in war's alarms', and the free variation on the melodic outline of 'from dim twilight to 'leven at night I shall not quit thy side'. (There are no bow-marks in Sullivan's manuscript, but it is always played *legato*.)

Ex. 131

The violins have an effective snatch of counterpoint, too, in 'Alas, I waver to and fro' —

Ex.132

— while in 'When maiden loves, she sits and sighs' the violas have their spinning-wheel imitation which actually persists throughout each verse with but two short breaks, although it appears only in a few bars of the vocal score.

Solo cello and double-bass steal a dramatic moment in the first-act finale of *Ruddigore* (following Sir Despard's line 'I claim young Robin as my elder brother!'), but in general Sullivan's treatment of the cello is less sympathetic than that of Offenbach, who was himself a virtuoso of international calibre before he had his first success as a composer.

Sullivan's operas contain very few numbers (other than recitatives) scored for strings alone — 'Ah, leave me not to pine', 'When a felon's not engaged in his employment' (both from *The Pirates of Penzance*) and 'He loves ! if in the by-gone years' (*Iolanthe*) are noteworthy exceptions. It must be remembered that his resources in this department were very restricted, perhaps only four first violins, two seconds, two violas, one or two cellos and one double-bass. The passage from *Patience* quoted in Ex. 36 (page 47) would sound admirable on a string band of normal dimensions, but Sullivan preferred to strengthen the first violins with a flute (octave higher), the second violins with a clarinet, and the violas with a bassoon. Even when all allowances are made, however, one occasionally feels that such doubling is overdone at the expense of clarity. Ex. 133 shows a transition from 'Were I thy bride' (*The Yeomen*). The scoring is appropriate and certainly not careless, yet one is sorry that Sullivan did not omit the clarinets or use them to replace the bassoons in the background; the first-violin octaves could have been given added power by being double-stopped (here quite practicable) in unison.

Perhaps this is hyper-criticism, and indeed Sullivan's doubling is often very judicious, as at letter W in the *Iolanthe* over-ture where the first violins (*sul* G) are supported by cellos, bassoon and (for once) two horns. But the fine string unison (unusual for Sullivan) in the introduction to Act II of *The Yeomen* is even more effective.

If wind instruments are frequently called upon to help out the modest string section, the reverse sometimes happens too. At the beginning of the second-act finale of *The Yeomen* the smooth semi-quaver alternations really demand three clarinets and a bass-clarinet; the flutes are already occupied and bassoons would here be unsuitable, but Sullivan manages very well by giving the lower half of each chord to the violins.

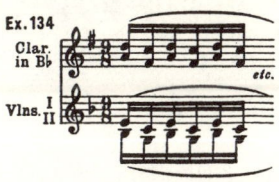

(A few moments later, the violins and violas add a fourth line to an otherwise unaccompanied trio for women's voices.)

Sullivan's string parts rarely present any technical difficulties, though they sometimes 'need looking at'. For instance a phrase that occurs twice in the first-act finale of *Pinafore* (as well as in the overture) —

— would be child's play to the first violins of a symphony orchestra, but is apt to be scamped in a provincial theatre; the desired effect might have been achieved more easily with a different lay-out.

A very striking feature is his addiction to *pizzicato*; almost every opera has at least one number that is virtually a *pizzicato ostinato*, the best of all, perhaps, being 'Kind sir, you cannot have the heart' (*The Gondoliers*). The abbreviation 'pizz.' is the cellists' bread and butter, but Sullivan's violinists also get their full share of the plucking, especially in the fairy music from *Iolanthe*. As an instance of contrasted *arco* and *pizzicato* I shall quote from that delicate evocation of Mendelssohn, the Nymphs' and Reapers' Dance from *The Tempest*; note in particular the smooth counter-melody for the cellos which keeps its own character while at the same time holding the whole passage together (Ex. 136).

Ex.136 Vlna.I (doubled in stretches by Fl. or Ob.)

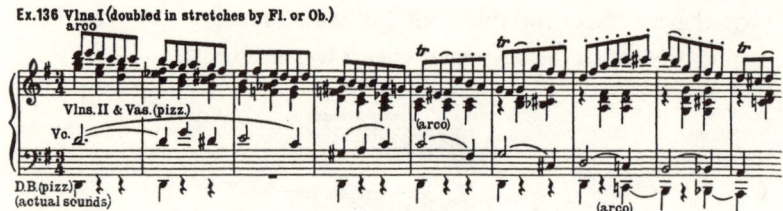

The child is father to the man, and by showing such a sure touch at the age of eighteen Sullivan set the standard by which his later achievements must be judged. His orchestration, at least, went from strength to strength — conservative use of the horns being after all a sin of omission only — and in this vitally important sector of the composer's art he deserves to rank as a master.

CHAPTER XI

SULLIVAN AS MELODIST

As the popularity of Sullivan's music is above all due to the memorable character of his tunes, it may seem illogical that a chapter on 'melody' should have been deferred to follow those dealing with his rhythmic, harmonic and instrumental resource. Is not the horse being put behind a train of carts?

It is true that trim rhythm, assured harmony, ingenious counterpoint and brilliant instrumentation will not save music from being still-born if the actual *tunes* lack the vital spark. But Sullivan's case is paradoxical. Streams of pure melody, *qua* melody, rarely sprang unbidden into his mind as they did into Verdi's or Puccini's, for instance. He suffered from too many Victorian inhibitions to be capable of such impulsive outbursts as 'Si, vendetta, tremenda vendetta' (*Rigoletto*) or 'Donna non vidi mai' (*Manon Lescaut*). Most of his best tunes owe their quality to the skill with which he superimposed a melodic outline — spontaneous perhaps, but sometimes comparatively formal — on a planned and often highly original rhythmic base. His method of composition being what it was, *rhythm* was the first subject to fall due for consideration, and Chapter IV gave plenty of opportunities for demonstrating this happy union of technique (rhythm) with inspiration (melody). The impact of harmony, counterpoint and instrumentation is less obvious but by no means negligible. Occasionally his preferences in modulation (see Chapter VI) cramp his melodies; elsewhere his addiction to simple chromaticism widens their range (see Chapter VII); a few of the 'double choruses' are palpably 'manufactured' (see Chapter VIII); and one cannot believe that the phrase from *Patience* quoted in Ex. 104 (page 104) or the eighteen bars following letter B in the 'Invocation' from *Iolanthe* would ever have been written if he had not had an oboe in his mind. It was essential to note such trends before attempting to assess his powers as a melodist. Consequently many of Sullivan's finest tunes have already been quoted or discussed and it is not proposed to go over the same ground again by cataloguing them here, but there are still a few points outstanding; these now claim attention.

Ever since organum first began to intrude on plainsong a thousand years ago, extraneous harmony or *harmonic association* has been used to heighten the psychological effect of a single melodic line. We need not go back to the middle ages for examples; the eighteenth century will serve. One very well-known air by Bach, for instance, has no chance to get going at all before the bass line forces itself upon our notice and becomes inseparable in our consciousness from the melody itself.

Ex. 137

Again, in the second movement of Mozart's symphony in G minor (K. 550) the tune *as the listener hears it* emerges from an overlapping series of repeated notes (on three different horizontal planes), while at the same time acquiring added character from the accidental bite in the bass.

Ex. 138

Some of Mozart's tunes, of course, are as capable of standing on their own merits as a good folk-song should be — but not all. A comparison of Cherubino's two songs from *Figaro* should make this clear. 'Voi, che sapete' would be perfectly satisfying if sung unaccompanied; 'Non so più cosa son, cosa faccio' wouldn't; the accompaniment — although discreetly subservient — is a necessary adjunct.

If a few of Bach's melodies (momentarily) and many of Mozart's (throughout) rely on such outside aid, it is not surprising that nearly all Sullivan's should do so. One can hardly think of a single one of his songs that would pass the searching 'Voi, che sapete' test. Possibly 'Oh, foolish fay' (*Iolanthe*) might gain a *proxime accessit*, although the rhythmic throb of the refrain — which is one of its noteworthy features — certainly needs pulsating chords to make its full effect. At the other extreme one might put 'Though tear and long-drawn sigh' (*The Yeomen of the Guard*). This is not a bad song of its kind, but the melody has little character of its own because — unlike any that Bach ever wrote — its *whole shape* is determined by considerations of harmony and modulation. If we transpose it to D major, we see at once that the first two bars are in essentials identical with the first bar of Bach quoted in Ex. 137 above (it is the difference in *detail* that emphasises the gulf between genius and mediocrity), but thereafter we are in a different world so that any further comparison would be ludicrous and indeed meaningless.

Ex. 139

In any case, Sullivan's 'harmonic associations' derive not from Bach but from Mozart; through these it is often possible to trace affinity in the formal vocal lines of their operatic numbers. A simple opening gambit used by both composers is a lead to the dominant (complete with seventh) followed by an 'answer' returning thence to the tonic. The melodies themselves are unaffected by the fact that Mozart's dominant sevenths are usually in the root position whereas Sullivan prefers to make the first one a second inversion.[1]

Ex.140a (The Magic Flute, *transposed*)

Ex.140b (Figaro, *transposed*)

Ex.140c (H.M.S. Pinafore, *transposed*)

*(The substitution of E♭ for the expected A♮ is a happy stroke)

Ex.140d (Patience)

Ex.140e (Patience)

Ex.140f (Iolanthe)

Ex.140g (The Sorcerer, *transposed*)

Based on the soundest classical principles, this convention is unexceptionable, but it offers so little scope that except in the hands of a master it slumps too easily to the level of a cliché; Sullivan did not overwork it, however. Verdi in 'La donna è mobile' (*Rigoletto*) and elsewhere developed it logically but inartistically by repeating the process in the immediately succeeding bars with altered notes, while retaining an identical rhythmic pattern; Sullivan avoided this pitfall except in a few border-line cases (*e.g.* 'When he is here' from *The Sorcerer*).

[1] For an interesting case where Mozart very nearly anticipates Sullivan's stock treatment see Dorabella's aria 'Smanie implacabile' from *Così fan tutte*.

By contrast, when the opening phrase closes definitely in the *tonic*, it may modulate to the dominant on repetition. Though less usual in the eighteenth century this formula was much favoured by Sullivan, especially in his early operas.

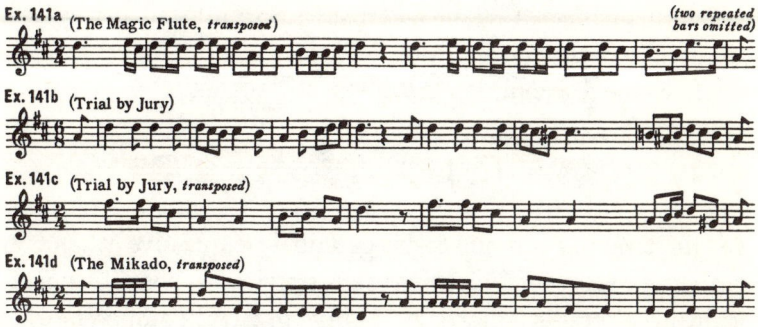

Ex. 141a (The Magic Flute, *transposed*)   (*two repeated bars omitted*)

Ex. 141b (Trial by Jury)

Ex. 141c (Trial by Jury, *transposed*)

Ex. 141d (The Mikado, *transposed*)

A rather more subtle effect is obtained when the opening phrase first slips into the dominant with a plagal cadence and only on the second time round settles there firmly by modulation.

Ex.142a (The Magic Flute)

Ex.142b (The Mikado)

Ex.142c (The Gondoliers, *transposed*)

Unfortunately, in spite of the other possible permutations of *varied* repetitions (many of which he used freely) and his regular excursions to the mediant rather than the dominant, Sullivan often started off by *exactly* repeating a short phrase (see Ex. 9, page 17). In a comic song this is a comparatively venial weakness (see Exx. 143 and 144).

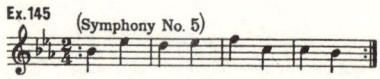

But in a melody meant to be genuinely expressive it tends to suggest poverty of invention or a striving — possibly unconscious — after 'catchiness'. Many greater composers than Sullivan have offended. Although Mozart rarely did so at serious moments (except in *Seraglio* where frankly some of the music is rather perfunctory), even Beethoven nodded occasionally —

Ex.145   (Symphony No. 5)

— and Verdi never threw off the habit. There are several instances as late as *Otello* and *Falstaff*, but perhaps the opening bars of 'Ai nostri monti' and 'Celeste Aida' —

Ex.146a (Il Trovatore)   Ex.146b (Aida)

— will serve as regrettable precedents for 'Love is a plaintive song' (*Patience*) and 'When a merry maiden marries' (*The Gondoliers*), to name only two numbers from Sullivan's operas where we have a right to expect something less banal. Here and there Gilbert may have saved him from such a lapse.

> The flowers that bloom in the spring, Tra la,
>   Breathe promise of merry sunshine —
>   [As we merrily dance and we sing, Tra la,]
> We welcome the hope that they bring, Tra la,
>   Of a summer of roses and wine.

If the line in square brackets had been omitted, it is quite possible that the tune would have incorporated a complacent repetition of the familiar opening four-bar phrase. The strophic irregularity, however, enabled Sullivan to maintain melodic interest throughout the stanza without losing the rhythmic lilt. (Cf. the corresponding second-act ensemble from *The Yeomen* — 'A man who would woo a fair maid' — where Gilbert wrote in jingling limerick metre and Sullivan promptly fell into the old trap.) The 'extra line' in Lord Mountararat's song from *Iolanthe* was also a boon to the composer.

> When Britain really ruled the waves —
>   In good Queen Bess's time —
> The House of Peers made no pretence
> To [intellectual eminence
>   Or] scholarship sublime.

As we noticed in Chapter VI, Sullivan's sequential use of the supertonic minor was rarely convincing, but here — under the stimulus of a five-line stanza — he was able to break away at (*a*) and bring the passage to a satisfactory conclusion.

Ex. 147

The process was repeated, *mutatis mutandis*, in 'When maiden loves, she sits and sighs' (*The Yeomen*), and indeed these two songs are good examples of how Sullivan's tunes sometimes develop well after an undistinguished start. Occasionally it is the other way round; an initially smooth melodic flow is for some reason forced into an unnatural channel, often involving — *faute de mieux* — an abrupt modulation to the dominant as at (*a*) in each of the next three quotations.

When *Iolanthe* was first produced, this chorus (as well as the entrance of the Peers) was accompanied not only by the orchestra but by a military band on the stage; it certainly has an appropriate vigour worthy of Sousa, which makes the letdown all the more noticeable. Possibly here, as in 'For he's going to marry Yum-yum' (*The Mikado*), the momentary weakness may have been partly *due* to Gilbert's metrical quirks. (Incidentally, why is the young lady always referred to in dialogue as *Yum*-yum? In this and other ditties Sullivan faithfully followed Gilbert's scansion and rhyming when he called her Yum-*yum*.)

In 'Never mind the why and wherefore' (*Pinafore*) the composer alone must be held responsible for the anti-climax. There is nothing 'tricky' about the words, yet although the tune starts splendidly — with an infectious rhythm more suggestive of Johann Strauss than Sullivan — it fizzles out completely after ten bars.[1]

[1] However it comes into its own in the dancing postlude; also in the overture.

In 'So go to him and say to him' (*Patience*) a similar Strauss-like rhythm is not only caught but successfully maintained throughout, and indeed many of Sullivan's tunes are very well balanced; 'Prithee, pretty maiden' (*Patience*), 'Ida was a twelve-month old' (*Princess Ida*) and 'In sailing o'er life's ocean wide' (*Ruddigore*) are *perfect* examples. Furthermore, they generally rise to a climax that arrives on time and sounds natural. (As Stanford rightly pointed out, this 'need not necessarily be a climax of height: it need only be the outstanding main feature of the melody'.) Because so many of his songs were in verse-plus-refrain form, Sullivan often had to contrive *two* climaxes, the second for preference at a moment of higher melodic tension than the first; the trio 'If you go in' (*Iolanthe*) admirably illustrates his skilful handling of this double problem.

However it cannot be too strongly stressed that melody-making is an art and not a science. Close analysis might disclose theoretical imperfections in many masterpieces of poetry, painting and music that have stood the far sterner test of time; we should not disdain any of Sullivan's tunes merely because they will not bear inspection under an academic microscope. The final judgment is one of taste, and even among his doughtiest champions what is meat for one may be poison for another. A song from *Haddon Hall*, for instance, which to most of us must surely appear as dull as ditchwater, is commended by the usually discriminating Dunhill for having 'a beautiful, indeed a distinguished tune'. On the other hand the same commentator finds one of Sullivan's 'worst indiscretions' in the 'appalling setting' of a trio from *Princess Ida* which the editor of the fifth edition of *Grove* singles out for special praise.

Even when one makes allowance for such natural variations in personal taste, it would be fair to maintain that most of the tunes in Sullivan's operas are good ones and very few really poor, though his inspiration drooped sadly after his break with Gilbert in 1890. Off stage he was less successful; only in a handful of the early works (discussed in Chapter II) did he reach the same standard under more independent conditions.

I do not wish to cavil at Ernest Walker's handsome acknowledgment of Sullivan's 'thoroughly *individual* tunefulness' (my italics), but in fact his melodic style *per se* is eclectic. It is true that he has certain mannerisms — *e.g.* a tendency to let a phrase hover round a single note over shifting harmonies for beats or even bars on end, and an overfondness for sharpened seconds and sharpened fourths as inessential passing-notes in a diatonic framework. But such idiosyncrasies are not peculiar to Sullivan; taken on the whole his tunes are more remarkable for versatility than individuality. It has been convenient to illustrate this chapter by several comparisons with Mozart, but his infectious gaiety often suggests Haydn and it may also be significant that he undertook joint responsibility for the Royal Edition of Operas (published by Boosey). This catholic collection ranged chronologically from *Don Giovanni* to *Parsifal*, and alphabetically from *Ballo in maschera* to *Zampa*; *Fidelio* rubbed shoulders with *La Fille de Madame Angot*, *The Lily of Killarney* with *Lohengrin*, and *Robert le Diable* with *The Rose of Castile*. But although Sullivan's melodic make-up certainly owed something to his familiarity with the standard operatic repertory of his day, his debt also lay in more exalted circles than those of Benedict and Balfe. When discussing his harmonic foibles in Chapter V four passages from *The Pirates of Penzance* were quoted (Ex. 42, page 50) to expose superficial resemblances to Schubert, Mendelssohn, Gounod and Bizet respectively. Though the *melodic* characteristics of these composers are difficult to recapture, it may nevertheless be appropriate to complete the picture with four corresponding examples — this time all from *Pinafore* — which to some extent at least again show their influence.

As before, however, the true-blue Englishman in Sullivan must be allowed to take his place in this international gallery!

In conclusion let me hammer home the point that I have been most concerned to make, namely that the quality of Sullivan's tunes — be they good, indifferent or bad — is hardly ever due to their melodic content alone; rhythmic variety is a large contributory factor although other associations (mainly harmonic) also play their part. Some of his near-contemporaries may have had as great, or greater gifts of melody pure and simple, and yet have failed to stay the course because they lacked commensurate technical equipment or consistently failed to achieve the refinement that characterises Sullivan's best work. When Sullivan wrote what we call a 'good tune' it was nearly always 'good music' as well. Outside the ranks of the giants there are few other composers of whom the same could be said.

CHAPTER XII

THE OVERTURES

ALL Sullivan's operas except *Thespis* (presumably), *Trial by Jury* and *The Zoo* were preceded by overtures or at the least brief orchestral introductions, although not all have been retained in their original form and one has been lost altogether. Most of them are essentially pot-pourris, but some are better compositions than that discredited connotation might imply, and a few are put together with considerable skill. It is generally acknowledged (though one expert, Boyd Neel, does not concur) that Sullivan relied to a certain extent on the industry of his conductors and other close associates. (The available documentary evidence was very fairly summarised by George Baker in an interesting article published in *Musical Opinion*, February 1955.) Nevertheless, one must always remember that he wrote the tunes, was no doubt largely responsible for the selection of self-contained passages suitable for inclusion, and put his name to the finished products. Bearing this in mind, let us examine their carpentry for traces of his own workmanship and mannerisms.

Cox and Box was written in aid of a deserving charity in the days before Sullivan knew such a luxury as a permanent musical director, and the overture is palpably his own work. As in the opening chorus of *Ruddigore* (and elsewhere) the key — G minor — is not properly established; at the fifth bar he settles down in the relative major and a long dominant pedal is needed to restore tonality for the subsequent — G major — section, which includes a passage astonishingly reminiscent of the 'second subject' from Schubert's *Rosamunde* overture.[1] One notes too that the coda — which is unusually Italian in character — is thematically independent of the opera. The brief introduction to *The Contrabandista* lasts only a minute or so and requires no comment.

The vocal score of the 1877 edition of *The Sorcerer* contains no overture, but according to contemporary press reports there was a 'light and melodious orchestral introduction'; the perspicacious critic of *Le Figaro* went so far as to imply that this had been borrowed from Sullivan's incidental music for *Henry VIII* which had been played in Manchester about two months earlier. When the opera was revived at the Savoy in 1884 with alterations and additions a new score was published, which incorporated the overture we know today. Nevertheless, there are good reasons for believing that it was in fact introduced at some stage during the original run at the Opera Comique. When working at terrific pressure to finish *The Sorcerer* Sullivan declined an offer of help from Alfred Cellier, who conducted and whose one-act piece *The Spectre Knight* shared the bill. But he might well have left to his colleague the task of constructing an overture once the excitement of the first night was over. And indeed, anyone who knows Cellier's compositions will recognise the hand of that clever craftsman in the short 4/4 *moderato* section; in the violin passages that decorate the trite waltz melody and the canon at the octave that adds to it a momentary flicker of interest; in the minor variation on the preamble to 'My name is John Wellington Wells'. By 1884, however, Alfred Cellier had handed over the Savoy baton to his brother François, so that if he wrote this overture — as I feel sure he did — it must almost

---

[1] It was in the *Cox and Box* year that Grove and Sullivan made their *Rosamunde* discoveries in Vienna (see page 13), but the overture — originally written for *Die Zauberharfe* — had long been familiar to British audiences.

certainly have been in 1877, although he evidently did not complete it in time for the first performance. It is a poor affair, but not all the blame lies with Cellier; there are comparatively few good tunes in *The Sorcerer* and what there are have unfortunately escaped inclusion.

The next five overtures in chronological order all conform to one type. They are pot-pourris in so far as they fall into three separate sections: the first cheerful and usually vigorous, the second expressive and sometimes sentimental, the third inevitably vivacious. (*Patience* is exceptional in that the first section is only four bars long.) It is the classical construction of the third section that entitles these pieces to be called 'overtures', for in each case it is in sonata form except that there is no 'development' to speak of — any more than there is in the overture to *Figaro*. Sullivan, when he employed assistants, no doubt instructed them to work on these lines; he himself had already done so in that introduction to *Henry VIII* which may have been temporarily on loan to *The Sorcerer*.

In *H.M.S. Pinafore* the third section is very much compressed (though still in miniature sonata form) and the dovetailing of 'Never mind the why and wherefore' into a short phrase from the first-act finale hardly suggests the workmanship of either Sullivan or Cellier. The overture puts one in the right mood to enjoy the opera because the tunes are good ones — two of them appear in somewhat altered form, very much to their advantage. Although Sullivan himself scored the opening, the donkey-work perhaps fell to Hamilton Clarke, who also arranged a brilliant orchestral 'selection' which Sullivan later included in a concert programme, thereby giving a boost to the Opera Comique box-office receipts which had fallen off alarmingly during an exceptionally warm summer.

Before leaving *Pinafore* and its overture, mention must be made of that extraordinary freak, its opening chorus. This starts, conventionally enough, with a drum beat, and then a rousing nautical tune — afterwards sung by the sailors — quickly establishes a key of no nonsense, C major. Just as we expect the curtain to go up, however, there is a modulation to the mediant minor, where to our surprise a plaintive oboe gives us the first verse of 'Sorry her lot who loves too well'. (When Josephine sings it later it is in 9/8 time; here it is imprisoned in 2/4.) After this closes on the local dominant — B major — the violins (still in 2/4) introduce us to Little Buttercup, soon handing over to flute and clarinet; meeting her under these conditions one would hardly expect her to blossom out later as a queen of the waltz. Nor do the bassoon and basses take kindly to the intrusion. They assert vigorously who *is* the Captain of the *Pinafore*, and although they do so in the improbable key of A flat minor, their protest encourages the violins and violas to remind the rest of the orchestra that up on the stage the sailors are waiting to start their jolly song. Buttercup makes a last despairing attempt to make herself heard in D flat minor, but the others have never known that such an outlandish key existed. So in a flash they all go back to C major on a good old ⁶₄, the curtain rises, and Her Majesty's Ship gets under way at last.

Now what is the point of all this? We have already had an overture of normal dimensions, and to have to listen at this juncture to a piece of symphonic development, however ingenious, rather tries our patience. One explanation suggests itself. This was only Sullivan's second full-length opera (with Gilbert), and although *The Sorcerer* had had an overture of sorts no precedents had been established; might he not have decided to dispense with a formal overture altogether? If so, this lengthy introduction to the opening chorus, with its thematically allusive and harmonically varied interlude, makes quite good sense. Then why was an overture afterwards added?

The simplest answer might be the correct one — second thoughts, for the overture was *played* on the first night although not published with the original vocal score. (Incidentally this included an unknown recitative which has always been given as dialogue.)

The overture to *The Pirates of Penzance* is longer, but much of the material is poor. (Nowadays it is sometimes given in a shortened version.) It was completed just in time for the first performance in New York, which preceded the London production by three months. Sullivan and Cellier worked on it together and I cannot guess which of the two discovered that 'How beautifully blue the sky' could be used as a counter-subject to 'A paradox, a paradox, A most ingenious paradox'.

Internal evidence ascribes the *Patience* overture to Sullivan himself. The four opening bars — where there is a character-istically abrupt modulation to the dominant — are never heard in the opera itself, nor is the charming *dolce* passage that follows, though it perfectly reflects the languorous mood later associated with the love-sick maidens. This shows Sullivan's touch unmistakably; so does the syncopated evolution of 'To doubt my inspiration was regarded as heretical' (*a*) in the sonata-form section.

The approach to the second subject at letter C is a hall-mark — compare it with the corresponding moment in *Di Ballo* and *The Yeomen of the Guard* — and the development section (all six bars of it!) anticipates a passage in the first-act finale of *The*

Mikado. In this sparkling piece one regrets only the use of cornets for the twelve bars of melody starting at letter A. During the nineteen-twenties an enterprising D'Oyly Carte conductor re-scored the first eight bars for strings only, leaving the cornets with a highly effective entry at the end of the ninth bar. But tampering with Sullivan's orchestration was frowned upon and the original version was soon restored.

An unusual feature of the *Iolanthe* overture is that it opens quietly. One could not better Dunhill's comment on the little wood-wind figure: 'even before we know its later application it seems to breathe the name Iolanthe'.

In spite of this early suggestion of G minor, tonality is rather vague until the five-note figure (*a*) — first heard in string octaves — leads to a subtle modulation and the 'cheerful' section then really gets going in G major.

In the third section, sonata form is handled more convincingly than in any of the other operatic overtures, though once again there is little attempt at symphonic development. Some of the music has no direct connection with the opera, notably the second subject (*staccato* triplets alternating between wood-wind and strings) which nevertheless evokes an appropriately fairy-like atmosphere. The refrain of the Fairy Queen's song is admirably combined with it in counterpoint, and later forms the basis of a rather abrupt return to the tonic (letter T *et seq.*) in time for the recapitulation. It will be noticed that a 2/4 rhythm keeps breaking in on the prevailing 6/8; it comes into its own in the coda, which closes impressively with a final reference to her Fairy Majesty. Sullivan took a lot of trouble over this excellent overture, rewriting it several times, and so far as we know received no outside help.

If the two sections of the introduction to *Princess Ida* had been followed by a third, this would have been the next 'overture' to discuss. One cannot help thinking that Sullivan must have intended to add a sonata-form section as in *Patience* and *Iolanthe*, but was prevented from doing so by the severe attack of his kidney complaint which occurred a few days before the first performance. Otherwise it is difficult to explain why this opera alone of all 'Gilbert-and-Sullivans' should have a comparatively short introduction leading straight to the opening scene. François Cellier, who by now was the resident musical director, probably arranged it as far as it went.

After *Iolanthe* the overture to *The Mikado* is disappointing. Some of the subject-matter, perhaps, is too closely associated in our minds with Gilbert's words to lend itself acceptably to orchestral treatment, and the construction is rather careless. The big tune from the end of Act I makes a fine coda, but nothing encourages one to dissent from the widely held opinion that the music was strung together by Hamilton Clarke. One is surprised, however, that a musician of his experience should have written the few bars quoted in Ex. 157. (A note-for-note transcription from the full score, making the necessary transposition in the piccolo, clarinet, horn, cornet and double-

bass parts. There is no overlapping except that the strings re-enter on the last chord, when it is too late to save the day.) If he was trying to emulate Glinka, who in the overture to *Russlan and Ludmilla* achieved a brilliant effect by contrasting the tone-colours of four orchestral groups in the course of a single bar —

— his attempt was a disastrous failure. Even if Sullivan's orchestration is sacred there is no need to revere Clarke's; might not the passage marked (*a*) in Ex. 157 be re-scored for *pizzicato* strings with perhaps a horn *sostenuto* supporting the second violins in the last bar? The experiment should be worth trying. (It is believed that Sullivan later sketched out a new overture for *The Mikado* on more symphonic lines, but unfortunately no trace of it survives.)

It would be ungracious to track down the perpetrator of the original overture to *Ruddigore*, which is a crude 'selection' hardly redeemed by its spirited ending. The final cadence is by no means typical of Sullivan.

In this overture a 'double chorus' (quoted in Ex. 74, page 80) is taken complete from the opera — an unsatisfactory move because it vitiates its effect in the proper place. Nor is the orchestration of the passage particularly skilful. The girls' share is given to cornets, with flute and first violins doubling the upper part an octave higher, and the men's line to oboe, two clarinets and bassoon in octaves. It must have needed careful rehearsing to ensure the correct balance.

When *Ruddigore* was revived after some thirty-four years this jumble was found unsuitable, if only because it incorporated two numbers that were omitted altogether from the slightly revised version then presented, and a new overture (which has been used ever since) was written by Geoffrey Toye. No precedents were followed and there is nothing Sullivanesque about it except the actual tunes ; if one of them is momentarily developed in a manner that suggests a haunted ballroom rather than a haunted picture-gallery there is no great harm in that.

Sullivan took his next opera more seriously than any he had composed hitherto, and conscientiously set out to provide an overture that should be worthy of it; all in all he may be said to have succeeded. The overture is an integral part of *The Yeomen of the Guard* and its main fault is an unusual one — there is not enough of it. Written in the course of a single night, it nowhere suggests that Sullivan was following his own precept — handed to Ethel Smyth — to 'make a shillingsworth of goods out of a pennyworth of material'. Here were enough musical ideas to last him for a quarter of an hour and he crammed them all into a bare five minutes. Basically the work is in sonata form, but where we look for 'subjects' we find only snippets, and we often have to be content with simple modulations instead of 'bridge-passages'. Nevertheless, Sullivan has been very successful in maintaining the sombre yet not too heavy atmosphere of the impressive opening statement of the 'tower *motif*' (Ex. 91, page 97). All the themes are drawn from the opera, but there are some subtle evolutions :

Ex. 160a

When a woo-er Goes a - woo-ing, Naught is tru-er Than his joy.

— for instance, becomes —

— and is later heard in diminution.

The development section starts very promisingly, but just as it is beginning to get somewhere it breaks off on a dominant pedal and is not completed until the same subject-matter returns half-way through the recapitulation. Such an unconventional procedure might have been successful in a movement of larger proportions but here it merely emphasises the lack of formal organisation. The climax leading to the coda, however, is very effectively worked up, and the overture as a whole can be regarded as a notable achievement by a composer who rarely staked a claim in the symphonic field. One is only sorry that he did not spend thirty-six hours over it instead of twelve.

The overture to *The Gondoliers* starts magnificently. The first section, lifted from a chorus in Act II, is bursting with vitality and has a springing rhythmic verve — reminiscent of Offenbach at his best — that is unusual in Sullivan. Moreover, the subsequent bridge-passage, where rapidly repeated figures on the strings alternate with emphatic chords on wood-wind and horns, is well contrived to rouse our expectations. For what ? We hardly know, but we certainly feel let down when an oboe gives its rendering of that rather ordinary little song 'When a merry maiden marries'. That this should be followed by the charming but here inappropriate gavotte does not surprise us, for by now we are reconciled to a mere medley. When the strains of the gavotte die away, we wonder idly what will come next. We are not prepared for an awkward hiatus, with conductor and orchestra waiting for someone to start the applause ! Truly never can the end of an operatic overture have been so ineptly devised. Sir Malcolm Sargent has decreed that when this point is reached the full orchestra should round things off with the infallible cachucha; one is still left with a feeling of regret that the splendid opening has never fulfilled its promise, and would gladly acquit Sullivan of being anything more than an accessory before the fact. But a note in his diary five days prior to the production reads: 'After dinner wrote, arranged and scored the overture, finishing at 3 A.M.' (He adds that Gilbert dropped in at 11.15 P.M. to discuss some final details; could this visit have put him off his stroke?)

Utopia Limited was preceded by a short introduction of about 120 bars (I am indebted to Miss Bridget d'Oyly Carte for this information), but none was published with the vocal score and the manuscript has been lost. After *Ruddigore* one feels that an overture subsequently disowned by Sullivan cannot have amounted to much; it may well have been an orchestral transcription of the last 118 bars of the first-act finale (letter Z onwards).

As *The Grand Duke* has lain almost forgotten for the last sixty years, any speculation as to who put the overture together may be considered academic. For the record it may be stated that it skims the cream — or should one say the top-milk? — of several innocuous 6/8 measures. François Cellier was still conductor and may have lent assistance, but one traces Sullivan's own hand in the concluding sonata-form section (the first of its kind since *The Mikado*); the second subject is in the mediant instead of the usual dominant and makes only a token appearance in the recapitulation. The overture is a better composition than any single number from the opera itself and might even be worth reviving for the edification of connoisseurs. The other operas of the nineties have only brief introductions of no particular significance; that to *Haddon Hall* incorporates a chorus which is sung behind the curtain.

Perhaps the fact that Sullivan wrote a few good overtures has tempted us to adopt too high a standard of criticism in discussing the others. After all one does not go to *Pinafore* or *The Mikado* in the same frame of mind as to *Fidelio* or *Tannhäuser*, and one should always preserve a sense of proportion. Ernest Walker's comment that 'the overtures are mere emptiness unless we know beforehand to what words the tunes will afterwards be fitted' really begs the question, and suggests a preference for independent detachable pieces like Rossini's; as it happens Sullivan followed the acceptable convention of Nicolai, Offenbach and Johann Strauss. The stricture of Sir Donald Tovey in his article on Music in the *Encyclopaedia Britannica* demands more serious consideration.

The Savoy operas live, and might, without delay to their popularity, have risen to the position of great music if Sullivan had had enough steadfast love of music to finish those parts of his work to which the public did not listen ; if, for example, he had provided his operas with better introductions than the perfunctory pot-pourris of their favourite tunes which he calls overtures and are quite as long as artistically decent overtures would have been.

Leaving aside the strange proposition that a composer might raise his status by concentrating on music to which the public does not listen and the evident fact that Tovey can rarely have attended performances by the D'Oyly Carte Opera Company (where the ritual of the overture is as strictly observed as it is at Covent Garden), the gravamen is perhaps justified. In this chapter, however, I have tried to acquit at least two or three of the overtures from the charge of artistic indecency.[1]

---

[1] It is remarkable how often Sullivan is at his best in the introductions to the *second* acts. In *The Pirates, Iolanthe, Princess Ida, The Yeomen* and *The Chieftain* there is skilful orchestral treatment or thematic development of the tunes we are about to hear on the stage, but in *The Sorcerer* (1884 version) and *The Mikado* independent material is used ; the passage that introduces the scene of Yum-yum's bridal bedecking is a self-contained poem in miniature.

CHAPTER XIII

A MIXED BAG

ALTHOUGH Sullivan earned most of his living and nearly all his present-day reputation by writing music for the stage, he had curiously little SENSE OF DRAMA. Most of the exciting moments in his operettas — and in *Ivanhoe* too for that matter — give us nothing more original than emphatic diminished sevenths that may be either *tremolando* or blasting. There is nothing intrinsically blameworthy in this — many of the terrific climaxes in Verdi's *Otello* (including the murder of Desdemona) are based on the same discredited chord — but Sullivan uses the routine so freely that it soon loses all force and degenerates to a threadbare theatrical convention. The occasions on which he handles a dramatic situation with conviction, applying his full resource, could probably be counted on the fingers of one hand. Dunhill cites 'Aiaiah ! Willaloo!' from *Iolanthe*, to which one might add the final section of the second-act finale from *Princess Ida*, the scene of Katisha's attempted disclosure in *The Mikado*, the short chorus 'Oh, day of terror !' from *The Yeomen of the Guard* and the duet between Rebecca and the Templar in Act II, Scene 3 of *Ivanhoe*.

Sullivan had a definite gift for CHARACTERISATION, but rarely fastened it on individuals ; although the music allotted to Mr. Wells, Dick Deadeye, King Gama and Lucifer (*The Golden Legend*) tells us something about them, it would be risky to invite comparison with Leporello, Iago, Beckmesser or even (Gounod's) Mephistopheles, and in truth most of Sullivan's principal characters are lay figures. There is little to distinguish

Patience from Phyllis, Lady Angela from Melissa, Buttercup from Dame Hannah, Alexis from Fairfax or Pooh-bah from Sir Despard Murgatroyd; some of the music might be interchangeable. That many of the parts were written for favourite players like Jessie Bond, Rosina Brandram and Rutland Barrington no doubt partially explains this, but the fact remains.

The variegated *groups* with whom Gilbert loved to people the stage gave the composer more scope; they can all be *collectively* identified by their music. There is as much difference between Sullivan's yokels and his gondoliers as there is between the Warwickshire Avon and the Grand Canal; the fairies of *Iolanthe* bear no more resemblance to the girl graduates of *Princess Ida* than Arcadia does to the popular conception of Girton in the eighteen-eighties. This flair enabled Sullivan to achieve admirable effects of both *contrast* and *unity*. In *Patience*, for instance, the dragoons are a perfect foil for the love-sick maidens musically as well as pictorially, while on the other hand *H.M.S. Pinafore* has a nautical tang *throughout* — not only in the sailors' choruses. The case of *The Yeomen of the Guard* is even more remarkable; here Sullivan achieved an *impersonal* characterisation, for the spirit of the grim old Tower indefinably pervades the music from the first bar of the overture to the final *dénouement*.

He applied PASTICHE with less consistency of purpose but nevertheless to considerable effect. Folk-music, as such, made little appeal to him, but he exploited some of its characteristics for his own purposes in 'Prithee, pretty maiden' (*Patience*), 'Now wouldn't you like to rule the roast' (*Princess Ida*), 'I know a youth who loves a little maid' and 'I shipped, d'ye see, in a Revenue sloop' (*Ruddigore*); the use of a Scottish harmonic formula to accompany the repetition of the word 'toddy' in *The Gondoliers* was a rather more subtle touch. Gilbert set him a rare problem when he drew on his memory of an old shanty.

What will you sing to me ? —
I will sing you one, O. —
What is your one, O ? —
One of them is all alone
And ever shall remain so.

In the *Yeomen of the Guard* version, like the original, each successive verse was extended by two additional lines (cf. *The Twelve days of Christmas*) and for once Sullivan was at a loss for either melody or rhythm ; eventually he was driven to ask Gilbert to hum his recollection of the tune. It must have been quite an experience to take it down from Gilbert's humming, but the result satisfied Sullivan who quickly saw the potentialities ; 'I have a song to sing, O !' became one of his great successes. As for the imitation Christy-minstrel scene in *Utopia Limited* (over which Bernard Shaw waxed enthusiastic), it will be hard to persuade those who have never seen the opera that it was anything more than an ingenious piece of fooling, possibly not in the best of taste.

A few isolated pieces suggesting the influence of Morley and Dowland were mentioned in Chapter VIII, but more often Sullivan caught an 'English' atmosphere by unashamedly adopting the manner (though not necessarily emulating the matter) of Purcell. The dance that follows 'When the buds are blossoming' (*Ruddigore*) is a very good instance ; others are the minuet (Ex. 161) and gavotte (Ex. 162) from *The Sorcerer*. Two other dances from *The Sorcerer* (one of the 1884 additions) and *Ruddigore*, although in a less aristocratic tradition, are also worth quoting from ; it should be pointed out that Ex. 163 is immediately preceded by an emphatic full close in E major and Ex. 164 by a chord of B flat major.[1]

[1] When I first heard *The Sorcerer* about forty years ago the number from which Ex. 163 is taken was replaced by a 6/8 country dance — very much in the Edward German manner — that was borrowed from *Haddon Hall*. Later revivals and gramophone recordings restored the 1884 version.

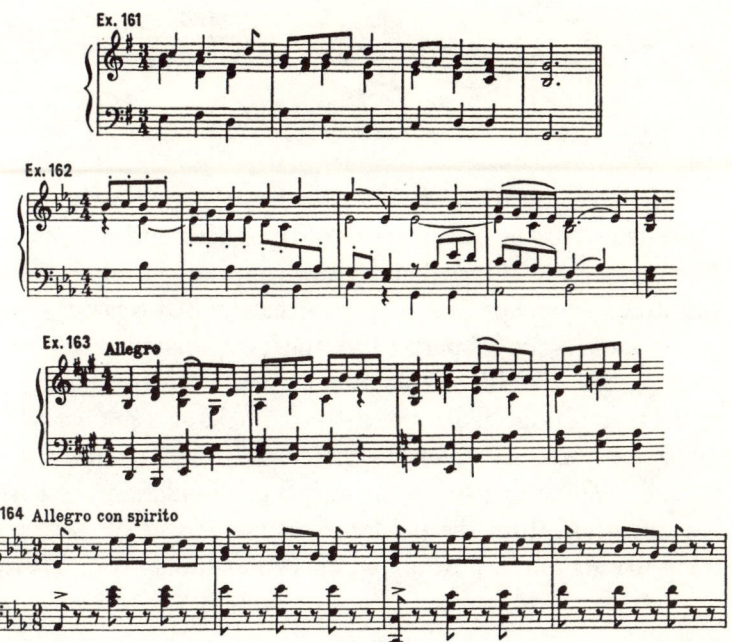

The gavotte from *The Gondoliers* and the 'drawing-room music' from *Utopia Limited* are in a rather different category, for here Sullivan added a touch of nineteenth-century idiom to the formal measures of the earlier period. He did the same in *The Grand Duke*, but though it is a pleasure to be able to quote a passage from that work without disparagement (Ex. 165) the vocal line is omitted because it was obviously inserted to conform with a ready-made orchestral pattern, which may perhaps have been lifted from one of the lost works of the composer's youth; it is far removed from his 1896 style.

We have already noticed how when pressed for time Sullivan FURBISHED UP OLD MATERIAL from *L'Ile enchantée* in *The Merry Wives of Windsor* and elsewhere, and he himself once admitted — perhaps half in jest — that he had treated *Thespis* in the same way. Apart from the girls' chorus referred to on page 88, it is difficult to trace any case with certainty, but in another passage from the first-act finale of *The Grand Duke* the voice parts are again so insecurely based on the natural melodic outline that one is prompted to speculation. Ex. 166a is a quotation from the published work; Ex. 166b (or something like it) might possibly be the original tune from *Thespis*.

Sullivan's student compositions (we are told) included a *Romance for String Quartet*, and one cannot help thinking that he must have drawn on this when writing *Princess Ida*. The libretto was a re-hash of one of Gilbert's blank-verse plays, so that the composer too may have felt justified in taking leaves out of an earlier book. If he did so, there is no cause to regret it, for in spite of some dull patches (for which the author must be held at least partly responsible) much of the music is not only contrapuntal in character but has the texture of chamber-music. No work of Sullivan's in that genre survives (a fact which itself could be significant), but surely a string quartet might have been raided for the benefit of Cyril's song 'Would you know the kind of maid'.

Ex. 167

The same clarity is noticeable in the opening chorus of the second act (see Ex. 52, page 64) — especially in the accompaniment to Lady Psyche's words 'If you'd climb the Helicon', etc. — and in the second-act finale a short solo for the Princess —

Ex. 168

— leads to a remarkable passage in which a phrase from Hildebrand's song is developed sequentially in the orchestra while conversation continues on the stage. It is hard to find a parallel in any of the other operas — except possibly between second letters D and F in the first-act finale of *Patience*. It is too long (and too elaborate) to quote in full; a few bars must suffice.

The trio 'Gently, gently' is even more suggestive, for not only are the voice parts obviously 'fitted in' — not very appositely — but from its construction one deduces that it might well have been the start of a string quartet movement. (If so, it was completely re-scored for the opera; it is here that one finds the bassoon solo quoted in Ex. 115, page 108.)

On the same type of evidence a passage near the beginning of *The Gondoliers* might also be the resuscitation of an earlier instrumental movement; the word-setting this time has been superimposed more skilfully, and the effect is charming.

The whole of this long and brilliant number has often been cited as an evocation of Italy and there is certainly plenty of southern sunshine in the twenty minutes of continuous music, but in point of fact much of it is more French than Italian in character — the opening, for instance, is reminiscent of Bizet's (very un-Spanish) cigarette-girls. 'For the merriest fellows are we' has an authentic Italian ring, however; so has 'We're called *gondolieri'*, though its roots lie in Naples rather than Venice.

In spite of Sullivan's Italian blood and German education, Paris and Monte Carlo were really his spiritual resting-places, and when called on by Burnand to set some French words in *The Chieftain* he captured the Gallic suavity of Messager.

Ex. 171

Nevertheless, he did not disdain the TRICKS OF ITALIAN OPERA in characteristic passages where *parlando* dialogue is carried on against a light orchestral background (usually strings only). Here are two instances separated by more than a quarter of a century — the first from *Cox and Box*, the second from *Utopia*. (As a detail, note the dynamic markings and the careful bowing of the first violin parts — nothing is left to chance.)

Ex. 172

Many of these Italian conventions, however, were quite foreign to Sullivan's natural mode of expression and he found there a fertile field for PARODY. An early example — 'A nice dilemma we have here' from *Trial by Jury* — is perhaps so much like real Bellini as to be an ape rather than a parrot, but in *The Sorcerer* he was more successful. For sound dramatic reasons the 'grand-opera' first-act finale was drastically curtailed in the revised 1884 version; this deprived us of an effective development of 'See ! see ! they drink !' (Ex. 174) sung a few minutes earlier as a straightforward trio (in both versions).

In reference to the parodies in *The Sorcerer* E. J. Dent wrote (in 1913): 'It seems as if a course of Mozart in English might be the best preliminary step towards educating our on-coming public to a really intelligent appreciation of Sullivan'. His point would have been made more clearly if he had written

'Verdi' instead of 'Mozart' and had applied it to the second act of *The Pirates of Penzance*; here Dunhill missed the joke when he disparaged the choruses of the policemen and pirates for their vulgarity. Vulgar they may be if taken seriously, but as a parody of *Il Trovatore* the scenes are extremely funny. The humour is sometimes obvious, perhaps, but nothing could be better of its kind than the chorus at the end of the fight when the pirates have overcome their adversaries. (Incidentally it takes some singing!)

Other conventions of grand opera were held up to ridicule in *Ruddigore* (Mad Margaret) and — rather more subtly — in two recitatives from *Patience* ('Am I alone?' and 'Sad is that woman's lot who, year by year') where Sullivan handled the absurd situations with technical assurance, but 'Poor wand'ring one' from *The Pirates* is little better than a caricature, because it is less skilfully composed than the favourite waltz-songs of Gounod which it sets out to lampoon.

Some apologists have attempted to excuse such quasi-religious effusions as 'I hear the soft note of the echoing voice' (*Patience*) on the grounds that Sullivan must have been indulging in the luxury of self-parody. It would be charitable, but illogical, to agree. Some of his early sacred works were admittedly sitting targets for such shafts, but Sullivan took them very seriously and it was not in his nature to push his tongue as far into his cheek as all that. It would be more realistic to urge in extenuation that he had grown up in the Victorian tradition of choral singing, and that having been year after year director of the Leeds Festival he always had those fine Yorkshire choirs in his mind. Their voices might well have mitigated the bad effect of the few indiscretions which he perpetrated at the Savoy. (And anyway, as he would have pointed out, the audience loved them !)

His upbringing led him to enjoy parodying Handel at his heartiest and he did so with competence, but the pieces sometimes sound incongruous in their context. 'This helmet, I suppose' is the best of them, but it is so glaringly out of place in the intimate atmosphere of *Princess Ida* that the intrusion jars. His knowledge and love of the works of that great master, however, also caused him to adopt the same style *unconsciously*; the concluding bars of 'Tell a tale of cock and bull' (*The Yeomen*) are surely spontaneous and not a parody.

Ex. 176

Often, too, the characteristics of early-eighteenth-century *recitative* are hit off to a nicety, but if Gilbert aided and abetted Sullivan at Captain Corcoran's first entrance in *H.M.S. Pinafore* —

Ex. 177

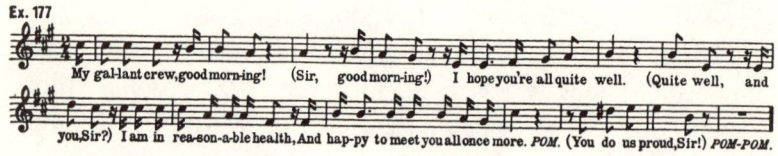

My gal-lant crew, good morn-ing! (Sir, good morn-ing!) I hope you're all quite well. (Quite well, and you, Sir?) I am in rea-son-a-ble health, And hap-py to meet you all once more. *POM*. (You do us proud, Sir!) *POM-POM*.

— Sullivan returned the compliment with his apt and memorable setting of the chorus entry ' What, never ? ' and later with the girls' *sotto voce* repetitions of ' he said damme '. Sometimes the fun was purely *musical* (see pp. 80–83, 90–91, and Chapter X *passim*); elsewhere he was content to point Gilbert's words with an inimitable touch while eschewing like the plague any suggestion of extravagant burlesque. In Chapter III (Ex. 10, page 21) a passage from *The Mikado* was quoted to illustrate how author and composer — in spite of their differing temperaments — could in conjunction evoke the quintessence of charm; except where middle-aged ladies were concerned they enjoyed the same *rapprochement* in HUMOUR. These are two qualities which play a large part in securing for the Gilbert-and-Sullivan operas their firm place in our affections.

At the time of Sullivan's birth		*Sullivan's age* at the birth of	
Spontini	was 67	Grieg	*was 1*
Auber	60	Rimsky-Korsakov	*nearly 2*
Spohr	58	Fauré	*nearly 3*
Rossini	50	Mackenzie	5
Meyerbeer	50	Parry	5
Donizetti	44	d'Indy	8
Halévy	42	Stanford	10
Lortzing	40	Messager	11
Glinka	38	Humperdinck	12
Adam	38	Elgar	15
Berlioz	38	Leoncavallo	15
Balfe	33	Ethel Smyth	15
Mendelssohn	33	Puccini	16
Chopin	32	Wolf	17
Schumann	31	Albéniz	18
Nicolai	31	Mahler	18
S. S. Wesley	31	Delius	19
Ambroise Thomas	30	Edward German	19
Liszt	30	Debussy	20
Flotow	30	Mascagni	21
Dargomizhsky	29	Richard Strauss	22
Wagner	28	Dukas	23
Verdi	28	Glazunov	23
Gounod	23	Sibelius	23
Offenbach	22	Busoni	23
Franck	19	Scriabin	29
Lalo	19	Vaughan Williams	30
Smetana	18	Reger	30
Bruckner	17	Rachmaninov	30
Cornelius	17	Schönberg	32
Johann Strauss	16	Holst	32
Brahms	9	Ravel	32
Borodin	8	Coleridge-Taylor	33
Saint-Saëns	6	de Falla	34
Delibes	6	Dohnányi	35
Balakirev	5	Respighi	37
Bruch	4	Ireland	37
Bizet	3	Pizzetti	38
Mussorgsky	3	Bartók	38
Tchaikovsky	2	Stravinsky	40
Chabrier	1	Bax	41
Dvořák	8 months	Prokofiev	48
Boito	7 weeks	Honegger	49
Massenet	1 day	Milhaud	50

CHAPTER XIV

A GATHERING OF THREADS

ATTENTION has several times been focused (especially in Chapters V, VII, XI and XIII) on the diverse influences to which Sullivan was subject; indeed, it has been impossible to exculpate him altogether from the charge of eclecticism. No doubt some readers have wondered where this was leading; they may have heard a piece referred to as being 'typical Sullivan', which now begins to look like a contradiction in terms. Is the expression then a complete misnomer? If not, what does it mean?

Before beginning to search for an answer to these pertinent questions, we must dismiss from our minds those instances of pastiche and parody that were discussed in the preceding chapter. They demonstrate Sullivan's versatility in a specialised department; most of them are appropriate in their context and some are admirable pieces of music in their own right, but they are no more 'typical Sullivan' than 'Im Mohrenland gefangen war' from *Seraglio* is typical Mozart, the gavotte from *Tosca* typical Puccini or the Popular Song from *Façade* typical Walton.

Sullivan's gift for group-characterisation must be taken into account, however. We can pass by the policemen's choruses from *The Pirates of Penzance* for these (as we have already seen) are a parody, as well as some of the country-bumpkin scenes from *The Sorcerer* which are little more than elementary paraphrases, though not all are as fatuous as the second-act opening chorus of 1877 (Ex. 178).

Ex. 178

Hap-py are we in our lov-ing fri-vol-i-ty, Hap-py and jol-ly as peo-ple of qua-li-ty,

Such simultaneous lapses by author and composer were fortunately rare, and as a rule Sullivan needed no such resort to impart a collective identity; most of his characterisations are as spontaneous as they are skilful. The Peers in *Iolanthe* really *are* Peers, the Japanese gentlemen of *The Mikado* remain throughout the opera the traditional embodiment of what Japanese gentlemen ought to be, even the court functionaries of the despised *Grand Duke* live up to their names; yet in every case the music carries a Sullivan stamp and the differences are those of character, not of style. The vague figure of 'typical Sullivan' begins to emerge from the variegated background.

The shadowy perception acquires more substance when we relate it to an advance in technical resource, a normal factor in any composer's development, but one which in Sullivan's case raises a complication because it marched side by side with an increasing tendency to infuse into his music the earmarks of a near-contemporary French school rather than rely largely (as hitherto) on the eighteenth- and early nineteenth-century classics. This undoubtedly caused the inconsistencies of style which were discussed in Chapter VII, but sometimes he managed to absorb the traits without losing individuality. 'A maiden fair to see' (*H.M.S. Pinafore*), which was characteristic of Sullivan in sentimental mood in 1878, led naturally through 'None shall part us' (*Iolanthe*) in 1882 to 'There was a time' (*The Gondoliers*) in 1889. In other veins the same process took him from 'My master is punctual always in business' (*Cox and Box*) to 'If you want a receipt for that popular mystery' (*Patience*) and from 'Let's give three cheers for the sailor's bride' (*Pinafore*) to 'Happily coupled are we' (*Ruddigore*). These are all 'typical Sullivan' of their respective periods.

The musician (who would anyway be unlikely to use such a phrase) will be wise not to press the notion further, but the man-in-the-street, who has no wish to talk about the early influence of Schubert or the later impact of Bizet (let alone modulations to the mediant minor or the use of the augmented fourth in cadences), knows a good tune when he hears one and knows that Sullivan wrote plenty, although he does not realise that they may often be subconsciously associated in his mind with Gilbert's words. One may look for — and find — features of technical interest in the Judge's song from *Trial by Jury*, in 'On a tree by a river a little tom-tit' (*The Mikado*) and in 'I stole the prince and I brought him here' (*The Gondoliers*), but what matters to nine listeners out of ten is that author and composer have here produced *entities*, in which the tune — when they hear it played by a band at the seaside — sets them struggling to recall the words, and the words — when they hear them quoted — immediately remind them of the tune.

Ex. 179

It is in such songs, therefore, that we find the 'typical Sullivan' of the popular imagination; of their kind they have never been surpassed and they are a worthy part of an immortal inheritance.

For the very reason that they are so well known and well loved, however, it is all too easy to exaggerate their importance when one comes to assess Sullivan's music as a whole, and in particular when seeking evidence of his influence on later composers. *The Quaker Girl* and *Florodora*, for instance, contain music which nobody need be ashamed to enjoy; unmistakably derivative, it often matches the artless *bonhomie* of *Tit-willow* and company, but no comprehensive comparison can be entertained because Lionel Monckton and Leslie Stuart had not a tithe of Sullivan's versatility, resource or discrimination. At one time Edward German and Sidney Jones looked to be capable of rivalling him in these respects, but German appeared to better advantage in symphonic music than in *Merrie England*, and though Jones' delightful *Geisha* had well-deserved success it is only as a 'period-piece' that it bears revival.

Between the wars one cherished a momentary hope that Sullivan's mantle might fall — how appropriately ! — on the shoulders of his worthy champion Thomas Dunhill. But although *Tantivy Towers* — which had the benefit of a brilliant A. P. Herbert libretto — was musically satisfying up to a point, it lacked spontaneity; perhaps the composer strove too hard to avoid obvious imitation of his idol. At any rate, for his next opera — *Derby Day* — Herbert turned to Alfred Reynolds, who for many years had been arranging the music of Arne, Linley, Dibdin and other composers of the same period in a laudable attempt to emulate Frederic Austin's skilful reproduction of *The Beggar's Opera* which had earlier had a tremendous vogue; occasionally, as in *Lionel and Clarissa*, he had incorporated new material which bore a superficial resemblance to the rest. *Derby Day*, where he adopted a less self-conscious style, caught the Gilbert-and-Sullivan spirit better than *Tantivy Towers*, but in the result it led nowhere. Gilbert's natural successor had tried out Armstrong Gibbs (*The Blue Peter*), Dunhill and Reynolds without finding Sullivan's counterpart; thereafter he gave up the struggle. Meanwhile two rather immature but exceptionally promising operettas were also played in London — *The Pride of the Regiment* and *The Jolly Roger*. Their young composer, Walter Leigh, might well have become the Sullivan of his day, but he was killed in battle in 1942 and lies in an unknown grave beneath the sands of the Libyan desert; it was a sad loss for English music.

How far Sullivan may have influenced more celebrated composers is problematical. It is astonishing how often the music of *Falstaff* brings him to mind (at the words 'So che se andiam, la notte' in Act I, Scene 1, for instance, and at the end of Act III, Scene 1). Verdi and he met more than once and it is just possible that the grand old man may have heard some of Sullivan's music on one of his infrequent visits to London; more probably he relied on a rare genius which enabled him to absorb instinctively the atmosphere of a far-away land of which he knew little and thus distil that same essence which was a natural part of Sullivan's heritage.

At home, Sullivan took no part in the ardent national renaissance led by Parry, Stanford and Mackenzie; conservative in his musical outlook, he gave little fillip to his advanced contemporaries, let alone to those who followed, except possibly Elgar (see page 72), Holst[1] and Ethel Smyth, to whom in her youth he was both neighbour and good friend. There are traces of his *method* — although of course the *manner* is very different — in *The Boatswain's Mate* and *Entente cordiale*, both of which might have had more success if the single-minded Dame had not insisted on writing her own libretti. Coming to the present day one thinks immediately of Benjamin Britten, whose catholic tastes and love of a good tune have drawn him to exploit composers of such differing styles as Purcell and Rossini; surely Sullivan, too, must hold a place in his affections. Much of *The Little Sweep* and the children's

---

[1] John Culshaw, in *A Century of Music,* suggests that Holst's first creative impulse derived from the example of Wagner, Sullivan, Stanford and Grieg.

songs, at any rate, from *Albert Herring* give credence, and am I the only listener who, when hearing *Peter Grimes* for the first time, was momentarily transported from the Borough to Tower Green?

The performing rights of the Gilbert-and-Sullivan operas, until 1961, are vested in the D'Oyly Carte Opera Company, the lineal descendant of the Comedy Opera Company which was formed in 1877 to finance the first production of *The Sorcerer*. It has maintained their reputation with a due sense of responsibility, but control has perhaps been too rigid; that the orchestral scores are not released for publication is a long-standing grievance with musicians. For the record: a touring company (at one time there were two) pays regular visits to London and other large towns in the British Isles, besides venturing occasionally across the Atlantic — it is always very well received on the other side. During the last sixty years all the Gilbert-and-Sullivan operas except *Thespis*, *Utopia* and *The Grand Duke* have found a place in the repertory (to which *Cox and Box* was added as a make-weight in 1921), although for one reason or another *The Sorcerer*, *Princess Ida* and *Ruddigore* have dropped out from time to time. *Utopia* and *The Grand Duke* have never been professionally revived in this country, but both have been given in the Dominions and the United States. Like *Haddon Hall* and *The Rose of Persia* (which made a brief reappearance in the West End in 1935), they still get an amateur performance now and again, and indeed amateur operatic societies are very much in the picture; many have an annual Gilbert-and-Sullivan Week, when the applause of the audience matches the enthusiasm of the players. *Ivanhoe* was revived by Beecham at Covent Garden in 1910, but today, except for 'Ho, jolly jenkin !' and 'Woo thou thy snowflake', is as dead as a door-nail. Outside the English-speaking world *The Mikado* has been played in countries as far apart as Russia and the Argentine ; many of the others in Germany and Austria at least.

Although most of the operas have had new scenery and dresses, often designed by contemporary artists of distinction, and *Princess Ida* and *Ruddigore* have been slightly revised, the D'Oyly Carte performances still stick closely to the stage traditions originated by Gilbert. Unfortunately they often fall short of what one has a right to expect on the musical side, especially in the vitally important orchestral department; even in London Sullivan's share is rarely presented as well as it might be. One therefore awaits with interest any developments that may occur when the copyright expires in 1961. Sullivan's music (so long as divorced from Gilbert's words) has been free for all since 1950, and fears entertained that this would lead to an orgy of jazzing-up and other misrepresentations have proved to be unfounded. Indeed the only event of significance has been the arrival of *Pineapple Poll*, a ballet arranged from Sullivan's music by the conductor Charles Mackerras, which is now given regularly by the Royal Ballet at Covent Garden and Sadler's Wells. Although the orchestration is disfigured by over-reliance on *glissando* harps and succulent counter-subjects for the horns, much of the music comes over well in its new guise, and the contrapuntal combination of a melody from the opening chorus of *Patience* with the second-act quintet from *The Gondoliers* is quite brilliant.

It seems reasonable to hope and expect that 1961 and the years that follow will again prove Cassandra to have been a false prophet. Indiscretions will be perpetrated no doubt, but they will be of small consequence if some enterprising management will concurrently undertake entirely new productions of the operas, supervised by directors of taste untrammelled by tradition, in which detailed attention can be given to the finer points of the music. Gilbert-and-Sullivan opera needs no new lease of life, but here will be an opportunity to ensure that its future is even more glorious than its past or present. (There has recently been an agitation for the copyright to be extended in perpetuity, presumably by special Act of Parliament. What an insult to Gilbert and Sullivan, whose achievements by now can surely stand on their own merits! If in this chapter I have implied criticism of the present copyright-owners in one or two respects, I am all the more ready to applaud their public-spirited repudiation of this preposterous suggestion.)

Although probably not a day passes without one of Sullivan's part-songs, hymns or anthems being sung somewhere, his more substantial achievements outside the operatic world are today almost unknown. Even *The Golden Legend*, which retained its popularity for many years, is now falling into a comparative neglect which is perhaps undeserved, although the other cantatas and the oratorios should be allowed to rest in peace. Some of the early Shakespearean incidental music makes an occasional welcome appearance, but of the more ambitious orchestral pieces the impeccable *Di Ballo* overture is now the only regular concert-goer. *In Memoriam* — so beloved of Sir Henry Wood — has dropped out of the promenade, but like the unjustly forgotten *Marmion* and *Macbeth* overtures it could do with an occasional airing.[1] (*Marmion*, unfortunately, was never published, though the manuscript score and complete band-parts — unused ! — are still in existence.) Finally the *Symphony in E*: the B.B.C. surprised us with an afternoon

---

[1] Since these words were written *In Memoriam* has been played at the Royal Albert Hall by the Hallé Orchestra under Sir John Barbirolli.

performance a few years ago; perhaps it may be repeated at a more generally acceptable time of day.

In view of the almost complete eclipse of his serious music during the last half-century, it is amusing to recall in retrospect that at one time Sullivan protested (and in his secret heart believed to the end) that only in such works as *The Light of the World* and *The Golden Legend* had he put forth his full powers as a true artist, and that the Savoy trifles were but a side-line. The side-line was a very profitable one, however, and 'art' soon began to count for little. Moralists may join with some of his earnest contemporaries in condemning this weakness of the flesh; posterity is grateful.

We are not concerned here with Sullivan's private life, but it is worth noticing how his music mirrors his personal character. Essentially easy-going and perhaps rather simple-minded, he never filled his head with metaphysical speculations, but was content to take life as it came and happily encouraged others to do the same. Indeed he suffered from an excess of good nature which, in his desire to please all and sundry, sometimes led him to follow the line of least resistance, to be unusually susceptible to outside influence, and occasionally to fall into the trap of insincerity. Small wonder, then, that his music too avoids extremes; we find no *Sturm und Drang* and but little wanton frivolity. He wrote down his ideas as they came to him, without analysing or caring about the source of inspiration; sometimes the result reflected his complacence, but how much more often his child-like acceptance of the good things of life that can be enjoyed by all who have ears to hear and eyes to see! This is not to say that his best music, even in the operettas, is all light-hearted; the scales are very fairly weighted. But while the good-humour is unrestrained, the melancholy is often tempered by wistfulness, as though the composer were subconsciously aware of his limitations in the expression of true feeling and dared delve no further for fear of disclosing them. Even in *The Yeomen of the Guard*, where an undercurrent of sadness continually ruffles the surface, profound emotions are rarely involved. We find the music by turns charming, genial, impressive; sometimes merry (though in this work there is little carefree gaiety), more often tinged with pathos or a hint of impending tragedy. But for the most part we remain detached; only here and there is a deep sense momentarily affected.

This inability to interpret human sentiments other than superficially precludes Sullivan from being named a great composer, in the sense that we apply the term to Beethoven, Schubert, Brahms or Elgar. To determine his true position is not easy. For one thing, like the disconcerting Berlioz, he obstinately refuses to sit in a tidy niche on the tripod of which one leg descends from the apex of Mozart through Cherubini and Weber to Wagner, another through Auber and Gounod to Fauré, and the third through Donizetti and early Verdi to late Verdi; this is because his music, as has been demonstrated, is a tantalising blend of originality and eclecticism. For another, most of his near-contemporaries of comparable calibre worked in restricted fields; to relate his achievements to those of, say, Hubert Parry or Johann Strauss gets us little further. *Prometheus Unbound* is unquestionably a finer work than *The Martyr of Antioch*, but Parry never wrote an operetta, and if he had one would be apprehensive. At the risk of precipitating a third world war, one is tempted to pit *The Mikado* against *Die Fledermaus*, but imagination boggles at the idea of Johann Strauss immersed in a Viennese *Golden Legend*. Yet we have to strike a balance between the eulogist who found Sullivan's operas 'as perfect in their way as the masterpieces of Beethoven and Bach' and the severe critic to whom his music was 'mere froth'. (The first comment was strangely misguided; Sullivan's operas are not 'perfect' by any standard — how many operas are ? If the writer really thought so, one could understand a reference to Mozart, but why drag in Bach and Beethoven ? Almost equally inept is an analogy with 'froth', which implies evanescence; whether one likes them or not Sullivan's tunes are still bubbling on after three-quarters of a century.) Let us compromise by deciding that Sullivan was a composer of talent who unexpectedly achieved greatness in a small realm over which he has since reigned almost undisputed.

As in the early days (at least) he did not take his operettas seriously, it may be true that up to a point his greatness was thrust upon him; but that was not its full measure. Gilbert and Sullivan, by eschewing coarseness and innuendo and making few concessions to the prevailing taste for trivialities, raised operetta from the level of the music-hall to that of the opera house, thus helping to change the climate of public opinion in its attitude to the theatrical and musical professions generally. When *Trial by Jury* was first produced, many good people still thought of a theatre as the haunt of loose women and disreputable men-about-town; a chorus-girl was regarded as little better than a prostitute. Fifteen years later the whole cast of *The Gondoliers* (chorus-girls and all) was royally entertained at Windsor Castle by Queen Victoria herself; the *volte-face* was complete. In this cultural revolution Gilbert was the instigator. It was he, not Sullivan, who cleaned the Augean stables; he, not Sullivan, imposed his iron will on a company of principals and choristers who were sometimes terrified and always respectful. As a creative artist, however, his contribution to the change of atmosphere fell short of his colleague's. The libretti, in which the complicated plots were as a rule neatly resolved by a stroke of quixotic but devastating logic, were so different from anything that had gone before that they were collectively an oddity, and oddities play little part in the long-term fluctuations of popular taste. (This is not meant by way of denigration, rather to draw attention to Gilbert's unique attributes; it is right and proper that his personal adjective should have found a place in the vernacular, a distinction which he shares with Shakespeare and Shaw among compatriot writers.)

Sullivan's case was very different; though he supported Gilbert in his rôle of unofficial Lord Chamberlain and encouraged him to be Lord High Stage Director so long as he didn't interfere with the music, he himself was neither individualist nor revolutionary; he carried on as nature bade him and did not realise that his own share in the proceedings was to have more lasting importance. Yet so it was: here was a fully-trained musician, a composer of contemporary repute in the field of symphony and oratorio, who developed his genius in a genre hitherto despised by the élite and normally the preserve of specialist purveyors who rarely had the inclination or ability to attempt anything more ambitious. That much of the serious music on which Sullivan's reputation in 1875 depended has died a natural death because it conformed too closely to conventions that were soon outmoded is beside the point. Although it might be kinder to his memory to ignore nearly all of *The Prodigal Son* and the *Festival Te Deum* (for instance), these and the other large-scale works of his first period have their significance, and, moreover, the technical resource which he acquired during their gestation enabled him when the time came to impart to his operettas a quality — for want of a better word one might call it 'musicality' — which set them on a higher plane altogether than those of, say, Millöcker or Planquette, whose *modus operandi* had never been tested in the refiner's fire.

By shining example Sullivan taught his own profession that light music can be civilised and scholarly without losing its wide appeal; that popularity, though a hazardous criterion, is not incompatible with artistic worth. More important still, he has bequeathed to the world at large a legacy which multiplies with the years, for every day young men and maidens are impelled by their spontaneous appreciation of his tunefulness, charm and humour to set out and discover for themselves the treasure-house of great music, thereby enriching their lives.

INDEX TO SULLIVAN'S COMPOSITIONS

GENERAL INDEX

(This index does not cover the chronological tables on pp. 18 and 154)

THE END

3 1543 50110 9310

750478

780.92
S949zh

DATE DUE

MY 12'79			
O 24 82			

Cressman Library

Cedar Crest College

Allentown, Pa. 18104

DEMCO